A Woman from Kerman with Memories of the Iranian Revolution

Homa Rouhi (Sarlati)

AuthorHouse™
1663 Liberty Drive
Bloomington, IN 47403
www.authorhouse.com
Phone: 1-800-839-8640

First published by AuthorHouse 4/11/2011

ISBN: 978-1-4567-4245-4 (sc)
ISBN: 978-1-4567-4244-7 (e)

Library of Congress Control Number: 2011902398

Printed in the United States of America

Dedication

This book is dedicated to the memory of my beloved late husband, Mr. Hesam Sarlati, a decent, intellectual, and honest teacher, husband, and father. He was instrumental in my education, career, and volunteer works.

It is also for my dear daughter Mina Sarlati (Fotovat) and her husband Mohammad Fotovat, both my precious supports in life.

Preface

It is not an easy task to write the preface to a book that was written by a woman whose life is so prolific. Homa Rouhi (Sarlati) was an important and effective player in contemporary Iranian history. She and her colleagues initiated the mission and set the scene for the current women's movement to the extent that we may say today's women's movement is a continuation of their efforts. If that was not the case, three decades after the fall of a governmental system in Iran, resistance for maintaining some of the provisions of the Family Protection Act ratified in 1974 (during the Shah's regime) would not have become a movement with national validity, the foundations of which were first laid by women from 1961 to 1976.

Today, supporters and even enemies prefer to turn back the pages of the history of women's rights development in Iran to January 12, 1979, or at best to a short period of time prior to that. However, the transformation in women's rights in Iran began in 1905 when the people of Iran decided to redefine the relationship among individuals, as well as the people with the government, through law. Since then, the law has been a standard by which to measure the differences between the rights of women and men. Certain well-known women gained attention; through calculated and peaceful means, they brought to the table the issues of discrimination for discussion and debate, and in certain instances brought the government to their side. Thus, about seventy years before the Iranian Revolution, the foundation of the women's movement was established in concert with the methods of the day, and has since overcome many rights and laws.Ms. Homa Rouhi Sarlati was a stable link who imposed her knowledgeable presence on these developments. She was a woman born in Kerman, who aspired that her peruse of justice be as soft and harmonious as a Persian carpet and enrich the fabric of contemporary Iranian history and culture in the same way. Sarlati was a very humble woman with a tranquility that she was able to maintain even in face of harsh revolutionary encounters; she was a very patient woman with enormous self control, who acted more than she spoke.

The history of Iran shows that Homa Rouhi Sarlati was a risk taker and always put forth her expert views in sensitive economic, banking, and industrial circles, several decades before the revolution. She was not afraid of what the future would bring. She gave timely warnings and pointed out economic obstacles. She was full of energy and, with patience, was ready to criticize the situation of the day face-to-face with government officials, herself being one.

Sarlati could have stayed in her position as high-level management and never entered into the field of fighting for women's rights, but she chose to fight for women's rights. When she felt that her presence was needed, she availed herself in the struggle for equality of women. She used the tribunal offered to her and entered into the field of women's rights and expanded it.

I first met Sarlati in the year of the approval of the Family Protection Law and the amendments thereto. At the time, I was a young, enthusiastic, and emotional girl that had read a few translated books about European women movements. Modern poetry was originally my interest in school. I gained some experience in political life, however, and entered the political society amid those who were enthusiastic and wanted to have more. Others were wondering like myself and did not know how to use their energy and interest in the right way.

In the intellectual atmosphere of Iran, many brilliant literary and art works were present. In those days, however, discussing the topic of women's rights was forbidden. If a woman dared to do so, she was teased to the extent that she was pushed to be silent or depart from the group. If somebody liked to speak about the subject, she first had to prove that she was somehow partisan of the Soviet Union regime; even so, the intellectual school would warn her that Proletarian rules came first.

Those groups did not satisfy me, but I did not fail to enjoy the literature and art works of my time. Emphasis on the leaders of the group was unbelievable to me. They wanted me to write only about natives in the United States. I did not understand why I should not write about myself, my mother, and my grandmother. Controlling rules were placed on the educated women who were interested in serious discussions about women's right in the political and intellectual atmosphere when the government annulled the democratic tools. Most women chose to be inactive and silent.

However, Homa Rouhi Sarlati used the capacities of the government in favor of women. In first years of revolution, her actions were blamed from every side. But now the judgment of people together with thirty years of experience is somehow different and evaluated as a very thoughtful movement. If the new judgment did not prevail, we had no meter to judge the new Family Protection Law submitted by the ninth government.

A few days ago, I visited Homa Rouhi Sarlati in her private residence. I reviewed her book and went through her albums. I found out that in her book she only revealed one aspect among tens of her historical presence. I prayed for her long life so that she could write more about her half century of experience.

Iranians have lost their contemporary history under the burden of political advertisement and economic hardship. The history of Iran is not only the history of Kings and Mullahs. It is the history of people among them and the people who made the change possible.

Homa Rouhi Sarlati is a role model, as they say in the West. She is a woman that has broken the social ideals by her own courage, and that of her husband. She was the first woman to reach the stage of high specialty in the fields of financial management, banking, and industry that had only been manipulated by men.

This book is a short story of an effective life. Read it, and find the character that is lost among propaganda and slogans.

Mehrangiz Kar
September 2008

Part One:
A Woman from Kerman

I was born on a spring day in the year 1925 in the Khajeh Khezr neighborhood of Kerman. My father, Razi Rouhi, was an intellectual and knowledgeable man who worked for the East Carpet Company. The Rouhi family was active during the time of the Ghajar Dynasty, especially in bringing constitutional law to the country. My father's family was all learned people. Dr. Mohammad Ebrahim Parizy, professor of history at the School of Literature in Tehran University, described Mullah Yousof, my grandfather, as, "Not an ordinary man. He was a high-ranking religious leader, a strong writer, excellent calligrapher with personal style, and economist with great views, and also an intellectual poet."

In my childhood, my grandmother was alive. She was called "Great Bibi." She was the wife of Mullah Yousof. Bibi Tahereh's father, Mullah Mohammad Jaffar, was a religious leader (mojtahed) and highly respected by people in Kerman. When he passed away, he was buried in the Tahbaghleleh Mosque - a holy place in Kerman.

The other son of Mullah Mohammad Jaffar was Shiekh Ahmad Rouhi. He was a very famous writer in Farsi. He learned Arabic with his father, and also knew Farsi, Turkish, and English. According to some, he translated *Haji Baba Isfahani, Jilblass, and Seven Edens*. Professor Edward Brown, the great specialist in Eastern history, wrote about him, "Between the three philanthropists, (Sheikh Ahmad Rouhi, Mirrza Khan Kermani and Khabirolmolk) the most honest person was Sheikh Ahmad Rouhi, who was well educated and a good looking man." Together with Seyed Jamalaldin Assadabadi, Rouhi was preaching the unity of Islam. He wrote letters to the religious Islamic leaders in Karbala and Najaf. His seal was the poem "I Fight for Unity of Islam, My Name Is Ahmad Rouhi."

In Nimrooz No.970 Feb. 2007, a weekly in London, Dr. Mostafa Alamouti wrote about the assassination of the three philanthropists, Sheikh Ahmad Rouhi, Miraza Khan Kermani, and Khabirolmolk:

> When it was revealed that they had cooperated in the assassination of Naseraldin-Shah and their relationship with the killer Mirza Reza Kermani, Mohammad Mirza successor to the Crown in Tabriz ordered their detention in Shehkelan - a prison in Tabriz. After two months in prison he ordered their assassination. Between the three victims only Sheikh Ahmad Rouhi proclaimed remarks against cruelty of the government in presence of Mohammad Mirza. Then Mohammad Mirza ordered to behead them

under a rose tree. They filled their heads with straw and forwarded to Tehran. They placed the bodies under a wall and destroyed the wall on them. Later Asefoldouleh uncovered the bodies, washed, wrapped and buried them in a public cemetery. This happened in June 1897. (No. 971, March 1, 2007)

Mullah Mohammad Jaffar had daughters as well. The most famous one was Bibi Tahereh, my grandmother and the sister of Sheikh Ahmad Rouhi. Great Bibi was a very authoritative woman and others counted on her. She was the first woman to remove her veil in 1935. She appeared in public without the veil, and other women in the city soon followed. In an old house in the Khajeh Khezr neighborhood at Kerman, my grandmother lived with my uncle Ahmad Rouhi (he was named after Sheikh Ahmad Rouhi). My uncle was a very powerful man in my childhood; he was adjutant to the army commander. His last position was as the mayor of Kerman. A loyal follower of Dr. Mohammad Mosaddegh, on 28 Mordad 1332 (August 19, 1953), when Mosaddegh was forced out of power, my uncle was humiliated, dragged on the ground, and dismissed from the job. He became disabled and isolated until he passed away.

My aunt Arefeh Khanom was a brilliant woman. She was compassionate and very kind, a sample of a good human being. She had three children from a failed marriage, and she raised them at the home of my uncle. My aunt cared about the neighbors and helped them as much as possible. She memorized thousands of Persian poetries. She learned to write Farsi on her own initiative. She always wrote the most poetic letters in her own way and used Persian idioms in her speech. Although working in my uncle's house did not give her any free time, she still studied and read books. Government authorities, neighbors, and family members all consulted her about their problems. She cared and loved children. When I was a little girl she taught me the poetry of Hafez and Saadi (famous Persian poets).

My father passed away after years of sickness when I was only twelve years old. My mother, Esmat Khanom Rouhi (Ebrahimi), was left alone with four kids, ranging from fourteen to four years old. She had no financial support and the burden of my father's debts. She was a hard-working, honest woman. A friend found her a job in the office of culture with a nine-toman monthly salary, and she became a teacher. It was arranged that the children's uncles would help her take care of the children. It turned out that only one of them, Ebrahim Rouhi, sent fifty tomans per month for the children's living.

I had a miserable childhood. I started going to school at age four when my elder brother Mahmood was going to a school run by English missionaries in Kerman. I cried every day, wanting to go with him to school. At last, the principal of the school accepted me. The name of the school was Doushizegan. The teachers taught us English and Christianity. Morning prayers and reading the Bible were our ethics. As I started to learn English, I loved it. After a while, however, the school was closed by the government and replaced with a public school named Seventeen Day. I continued my education in that school.

When I was ten years old, Reza Shah ordered compulsory removal of the veil for Iranian women. Wives of government employees and leaders removed their veils in the public and participated in the celebrations and lectures. The prejudiced Muslim men, however, did not allow their wives to go out of home without a veil. Some women were scared of their husbands, and others believed that a woman without veil was unchaste and should stay at home for life. Memories of those exciting days are still vivid in my head. I was so attracted to women who dared to stand before the public and talk about the freedom of women.

My education continued through until ninth grade at Kerman. Then, my mother decided to move to Isfahan to live with her father. My grandfather, Mohammad Sadegh Ebrahimi, was a learned, liberal judge. Every once in a while he was transferred to a new province. In Isfahan, I continued my education at Behesht Aeen School, which was run by English missionaries. In addition to the ordinary curriculum, they taught English texts. I progressed in English and was eventually able to obtain an English proficiency certificate from Cambridge University. My mother continued her job in Isfahan. She was teaching in a school at Jolfa. Every day she rode a bicycle from Isfahan to Jolfa. My grandparents were not very happy being responsible for a family of five, but they had no choice.

My grandfather was later transferred to Shahrood. As there was no girls' secondary school, I was sent back to Kerman to get my high school diploma. My elder brother Mahmood was seriously ill and was sent to a rehabilitation center in Tehran. My mother and younger sister went to Shahrood. My younger brother Javad stayed at Kerman. The family was all scattered. My sister Farzaneh passed away in Shahrood when she was fourteen, and then I was sent to Shahrood to live with my mother. This was the best time of my life. I was the only girl there with a high school diploma.

However, I was not yet eighteen years old and could not have a job. I taught as a volunteer at schools and started teaching private English classes, making some money for myself.

In Shahrood, Hesam Sarlati, a friend and follower of my grandfather, asked for my hand in marriage. He had gone to Shahrood to consult with my grandfather about marriage to a girl from his own family. When he saw me, he changed his mind. In a letter to his father, he expressed his willingness to marry me. His father wrote a letter to my grandfather about the case. My grandfather, who was an intellectual man, asked my views. I felt that it was time to depart, and, as I knew my future husband and his family, I agreed with the marriage.

My future husband was a graduate from Tehran University in the field of biology. He worked as a high school teacher in Sary, north of Iran. He first needed some time to save money for the marriage. At this time, my grandfather was transferred from Shahrood to Tehran, and our hard time started in Tehran. I tried to find a job. I applied to Bank Melli Iran and the National Oil Company. Both approved my application because of my high grades and certificate in English. My grandfather preferred my working in an Iranian organization, however, rather than the oil company, which was under the management of an English company.

I started my job at the bank in January 1943. My first assignment was in the office of money control. I tried to do more than just my own job, which was typing letters. One time I was punished because I was writing the book of old bank notes to help a colleague.

Employees of Bank Melli Iran had very good benefits, and they were better off than the other government employees. My first salary at the bank was ninety tomans a month. In two months' time, I got a raise and could buy myself good clothing.

Around that time, my elder brother Mahmood became seriously ill. My mother helped him very much, but it did not work, and he died at age eighteen. My younger brother went to military school and married a relative. His whole life he worked for the department of education.

In 1995, he passed away after his wife (Ghamar Khanom) and his young son, Abbas, died. My brother's daughters, Zohreh, Sohayla and Maryam, are very capable persons, good wives, and caring mothers.

Soon it was time for my marriage. My husband transferred to Isfahan, where his home and family were. We had a wedding ceremony in Tehran. The next day we started our trip to Isfahan. One night we stayed at Ghom (a city near Tehran), and the next day we were on our way to Isfahan. The roads were dusty, and the bus that carried us for two days to reach Isfahan was very old. Our matrimonial life started in an old, inherited house in the Sarlat neighborhood. My husband's grandmother lived with us. She was a very kind and caring woman and managed our household.

My husband was a very liberal man with high humanistic morals. I knew no other man that believed in equality between a man and woman as he did. He encouraged me in my education and social activities. As I am writing this memoir, it has been two years since he passed away in June 2006 when he was ninety-two years old. In his last year of life, he became very ill and suffered very much. He is buried in the beautiful North York Cemetery in Toronto, Canada.

The late Hesam Sarlati compiled and printed a

164-years comparative calendar in two volumes: one from 1841 to 1881, the other from 1881 to 2004. In the preface of the book, it is said that there was a great need for a calendar to compare the solar, lunar, and Gregorian dates existing in documents. Unfortunately, there was no such source; the available ones were not authentic and had errors in the base of their calculations. By using old calendars and newspapers in the Parliament library, such as *Vaghye Etefaghieh* (an Iranian newspaper), the *National Gazette*, and the *Melli newspaper*, this calendar was complied. In the calendar, each solar year came in a separate page, and the first day of the solar month is compared with the lunar and Gregorian days. The calendar has a separate column for solar months before 1925 that were called the house of Zodiac (Borouje Falaki). By using this calendar, it is easy to find out what special day in the solar year corresponds with that day in the Gregorian or lunar calendar.

****

Now I will talk about the greatest loss in my life. My son Razi Sarlati was educated in the United States and graduated from Lehigh University. He worked at the Beckthel Company, a manufacturer of atomic power stations. Razi married Marion Lyon, an American girl, and they were a happy couple. After ten years at Beckthel, he retired early and started his own business. When he was forty-five, he suffered from Hodgkin's disease and leukemia, and passed away. He has two sons, Kamran and Bijan. Kamran graduated college and works in Chicago. Bijan is studying industrial psychology at a school in Pennsylvania.

****

I was transferred to the Isfahan Bank Melli. In those days, women worked mostly in education. It was unusual for a woman to work at a government office. My office was in a faraway corner of the building with a private exit. At this time, my first child Mina was born. Her birth was in an English hospital, which was not very well equipped. Patients had to bring their own necessities. After two days of labor, Mina was born, a beautiful and healthy child that talked and walked very soon.

I decided to move to Tehran, as I liked the city better than Isfahan. It was a difficult job and everybody was shocked. My husband, who wanted me to be happy, agreed with me and sold his inherited house. In Tehran we built a house in Gholhak, a neighborhood with bus service once every hour. My husband, daughter, and I, resided at my grandfather's residence while the house was being built. My grandmother, Mahtalat Khanom, took care of my child while I was at work. It was a hard time. My grandparents, my uncle Mehdi, my husband, my child, and I, were all living in a small house. At this time, another relative, whose husband had abandoned her and left her with no place to live, joined us as well. It was a tough time, but we all practiced understanding and cooperation.

My transfer to Tehran was difficult. They asked me to find a worker in Tehran to replace my position in Isfahan. I did that, and upon my return to Tehran, they placed me in the Bank Melli Bazzar branch, which was a terrible, dark place in a downtown passage. On hot summer days when the power was cut, they lit the place with kerosene burner lamps. Eventually, a new bank building was finished and Bazzar Bank

Melli transferred to the new location. A manager in the bank was appointed to the job of vice presidency in the central office and agreed with my request for transfer to the head office. My first appointment was in the credit department, where I received the right of signing bank documents, which was very unusual for women. My signature was introduced to all banks and correspondents in Iran and abroad.

While I was working at the bank, I was attending the College of Banking. I attended night classes to obtain a diploma that was good for a university. For three years, I studied at night. I then took the entry exam for Tehran University and was admitted into three fields. I chose the school of law, as I wanted to work as a lawyer to help women. In the school of law, attendance was not compulsory, and it was possible for me to learn the curriculum outside the classroom and still pass the examinations.

It was the policy of Bank Melli Iran to give a one-hundred-tomans raise to an employee who was able to receive a Bachelor of Arts degree. My narrow-minded boss did not let me use my leave for passing an exam. They reasoned that bank employees should use their leave for relaxing in order to be ready for more work.

As I had very limited opportunity for attending classes, I studied the law texts with my grandfather. The professor once asked me why I was not attending his classes. I told him that I was working my job, but I was learning my lessons. He told me that the students that attended every class did not know anything, and he questioned how I could know anything. I insisted that I was learning, and he let me answer several questions that the other students were not able to answer.

In the year 1960, Bank Melli Iran held an exam

for sending employees to attend training at foreign banks. I applied for the training for a few years in a row. Each time they told me that the position was for a male employee. Finally, however, a bank vice president allowed me to take part in the exams. The bank was certain that no woman was capable of doing the job. I passed the exam, and thus was the first woman in Bank Melli to be sent abroad for training.They discriminated against me, however, and sent me to a college instead of to a bank. This was still a good opportunity for me. My husband signed the agreement to support me, and I left my two children with him and their grandmother and followed my destiny.

By recommendation of the British embassy, I was sent to St. Godric's College in London, the best girls' college in the city. I finished the two-year course in one year and three months. I studied banking, shorthand, typing, accounting, and English correspondence. Once back in Iran, I was made secretary to the president of the bank. This had previously been a job for high-ranking and experienced men.

After a few months, they assigned me to the branch of Bank Melli Iran at 1 Wall Street in New York. It was a very difficult experience, because I took Mina, twelve years old, and Razi, four years old, with me. My husband stayed in Tehran. In a big city like New York, I knew nobody except the chief of the bank branch. My first problem when I got there was to find an apartment. Nobody wanted to rent an apartment to a newcomer with two children. For a while, we lived in a boardinghouse. Eventually, an Iranian lady rented me her apartment while she went back to Iran. The apartment was in a very crowded and poor neighborhood. I changed my home many times, and every time I lost a month of payment.

Mina was very smart and found her own way. She continued her education without losing any credit. She took care of herself and her brother. We worked at home together, and when possible, visited the interesting sites in New York. My home was very far away from my office. Every day I had to travel two hours by express train.

My grandfather passed away in Tehran and my mother became lonely. I supported her so that she could come to the United States and live with us. She was left alone at home, was not feeling well, and did not know English, yet still she faced her life in good spirit. With my mother's presence, our life changed and improved.

As there was not much work to do at the Bank Melli New York branch, I was assigned to the Iranian Economic Mission in Washington, DC. It was a new job, new city, and new problems with strange people and colleagues. Once again, the main problem was finding an apartment. I found one eventually, two towns away in Falls Church, Virginia. The bus service was once an hour.

In the Iranian Economic Mission, each government organization had one or two representatives. Larijani and I were representatives of the Central Bank of Iran. The chief of the mission was Dr. Jahangir Amuzegar, a professor of economics at American University. He was a very intelligent man, but his manners were not good. He was autocratic, taking the best opportunities, and did not care for the well being of his staff. In Washington I was introduced to the Iranian Mission at the United Nations and the Iranian consulate. I worked for them whenever they needed my services.

My husband was able to take a leave of absence from his work and joined us in Washington. This made us very happy, and it was very convenient.

After four and a half years of living in the United States, I decided to go back to Iran. This was around the time that Mina finished high school. I enrolled her in Dambarton Girls College. Razi, my mother, and my husband returned to Iran. With my savings, I embarked on a trip around the world with a friend. The final part of my trip was to India and Pakistan. Once I saw the poverty in those countries, I was happy to go back to my home country.

The Central Bank of Iran separated from Bank Melli Iran, and I started my job as part of the research staff in the Center for Attraction and Protection of Foreign Investments in Iran. I helped an American professional compile a guide for investment in Iran. He was traveling between Tehran and New York. Every time he was in Tehran, he handed me a list of materials he wanted to include in the guide. I collected and translated them for him. At the same time, I started as a board member for a recreation club for the personnel of the Central Bank of Iran.

Upon my return from the United States, I decided to continue my education. I enrolled in courses for a Master of Business Administration (MBA) and graduated in 1970.

In the middle of all of that work, I translated a book for youths, *Call it Courage* by Armstrong Sperry. The book was printed by the Amir Kabir Publishing Company and was recognized by the Council of Children's Books as the best translation of the year. All three thousand copies were sold out in a very short time.

I worked as a trustee at Farah Pahlavi (Alzahra) University and as a board member of the National Institute for Protection of Children and the International Women's Lawyers Association during the presidency of

Dr. Mehragiz Manoucherian. It was at this time that an organization was established by Princess Ashraf Pahavi (the Shah's sister) named the Iranian Women's Organization; it was an umbrella organization for all women organizations in Iran. Up to this point, volunteer work had only been performed by high-class women and those close to the royal court.

Women's rights had progressed, and women were studying all fields of education and participating in every possible activity. However, Princess Ashraf was not happy with the performance of the Women's Organization and wanted to bring young, well-educated women into the organization. To meet this goal, she asked the cabinet ministers to introduce competent ladies into the organization. A few suitable women were introduced to her.

The princess selected me to be the secretary general of the Women's Organization. I was young and had no experience in social works or dignitaries to support me. My appointment was a surprise, and people wondered where I came from and who introduced me to the princess. The board of directors was also selected in the same manner.

In a short period of time, I activated the organization with very interesting plans, such as a Center for Family Protection in different cities. These centers provided literacy classes, legal aid, daycare for children, and vocational training. The Women's Organization started daycare in different ministries for working mothers by inclusion of expenses in the government budget. The organization established a school for training social workers to help families in rural areas.

The Family Protection Law which was introduced by women lawyers, such as Dr. Mehragiz Manouchehrian, who faced problems when working in the courts. By the cooperation of judges working in family courts, the organization amended the law in a seminar and introduced it to Parliament.

While in the position of secretary general of the Women's Organization, I traveled to different cities and talked to women about their problems in order to find solutions for them. Working in the Women's Organization was not an easy job, but it was a great experience for me and the best time for Iranian Women to participate in all walks of life. After two years in the position, Simin Rejali was appointed as secretary general. I was exhausted and was thinking of leaving that field of activity for good. Because of the majority of votes and recommendation of the princess, I continued as a board member of the organization and continued to support Iranian women until the day of the revolution when everything flipped upside down.

After being secretary general of the Women's Organization, which was a full time job, I was assigned to the position of director general of foreign trade in Europe and the United States at the Ministry of Economy. In this position, I traveled to different countries and participated in international conferences and negotiations. When on international trade missions, my position was surprising to the rest of the delegates, and they were appreciative of women's advancement in Iran.

Those were the years of enhancement for Iranian women's rights. Women held the titles of minister, deputy minister, MP, senator, judge, lawyer, director, professor, and physician. They were admitted to high jobs in the government and showed their capabilities. In these years, two women were appointed as ministers. Mahnaz

Afkhami was the minister in charge of women's affairs. She was outside of Iran during the revolution which saved her life. The other woman was Dr. Farokhroo Parsa, the minister of education, who was executed in the first year of the Islamic Revolution in a very nasty manner. The story of her life and works is compiled in a book by Mansureh Pirnia, *Lady Minister.*

At this time, the Ministry of Economy was divided into three ministries: the Ministry of Industries and Mines, the Ministry of Economy, and the Ministry of Commerce. I was appointed to the Ministry of Commerce, the director general of foreign trade. I was not happy with this job because of the unlawful and hasty decisions made by the minister, which pleased only the enemies of the regime.

Farideh Diba, Shahbanou Farah's mother, a very respectful and benevolent lady, asked me to work in her office. This office responded to the requests of needy people. The ceremonial affairs were handled by Mahin Hasheminejad, a close companion. I was not very busy at the job. The two years I was there were very relaxing; the work was just ceremonial.

This was also the time when public protest started. People were complaining about the officials and some asked for financial support. Farideh Diba was working as president of many charitable organizations and was the vice president of the Iranian Women's Organization. She helped people as much as possible. The lower staff of the royal court who received better pay than many government employees were soon taking advantage of her kindness.

While working with Farideh Diba, we took a trip to Romania. Their reception was glorious, and the sightseeing was very pleasant. The Iranian Mission met Nicolae Ceaușescu, the president of Romania. A short time after our return to Tehran, he and his wife were executed by the people.

Princess Ashraf, president of the Iranian Women's Organization, appointed me as an Iranian representative in the Commission on Status of Women in the United Nations. The Iranian government was very generous with helping international bodies; a great donation was promised to the United Nations for the establishment of a center of information for women. The Iranian mission was highly respected, and when we discussed the financial grants of our government to the women's movement, they were surprised.

The Iranian Women's Organization was a powerful and influential organization. The budget was secured by the sale of textbooks that were printed by the Royal Services Organization. The organization's budget distributed money to women's organizations in the provinces.

Farokh Najmabadi, the minister of Industries and Mines, asked for my biography in order to introduce me to the State Administration and Employment Organization as a nominee for the deputy minister in charge of Parliament and Administrative Affairs. I was selected for the job and introduced to the Shah in February, 1976. Subsequently, I was attending the sessions of Parliament and managed the administrative affairs of the ministry. The Ministry of Industries and Mines was a great ministry with many affiliations. Defending the budget of the ministry and the affiliates in Parliament was a difficult task.

While in this position, I rendered many services for helping the employees with their promotion and retirement orders issued by other ministries. I started a cooperative fund and a lending system. Lunch was provided with the best quality and price, and for their breaks, they were given tea, coffee and pastries. The minister and the other authorities would do whatever possible to satisfy the employees.

This was the beginning of protests of opposition. No matter what was done for people, they still asked for more and tried to cripple the government. They were making statements against the government and wanted democracy. Every day the debates became hotter, and Hovayda, the prime minister, gave them privileges in order to silence them.

In the change of cabinet, the minister of Industries and Mines was changed. As was routine, the deputy minister resigned to let the new minister make his own choice. The new minister, Dr. Reza Amin, appointed me as his deputy minister. Mr. Amin was a hard working, skilled manager and a very humble person. He increased my authority, which included spending the secret budget at his disposal for helping the specialists who came from abroad and did not fit within the normal salary schedule of the government. I was very obsessed about spending the budget. When the revolutionary people broke through the ministry and got into the safe, books, and money inside, they could not find any failure in the accounts.

Gradually, the opposition was organized, and every day they had strikes and demonstrations. They wanted to dethrone the Shah and topple the government.

I started to write down my memories from the revolution when the demonstrations started. Thirty years have passed since the revolution. I compiled this book so that the memories would not loose their effect. I wanted to remember the events of those days in the same way that they happened, which may provide for a better judgment of the revolution.

The Shah of Iran's Birthday celebration. Homa Rouhi and the deputy ministers of the Ministry of Industries and Mines. September 26, 1977

Homa Rouhi, Mahnaz Afkhami, and Heshmat Yousofi in Moscow meeting with Nina Treshkova, the first woman in space. April 1956

Homa Rouhi as chairperson at the United Nations Conference on the Status of Women. March 1978

Princess Ashraf Pahlavi recognizing services of Homa Rouhi to Iranian women. February 26, 1977

Shahbanou Farah Pahlavi at the Iranian New Year celebration.

Homa Rouhi at the Iranian Management Association

Homa Rouhi at the International Council of Women

From Left: Razi, Marion and Kamran Sarlati; Nima, Sahba, Salma, Mina and Mohammad Fotovat. Sitting: Hesam and Bijan Sarlati and Homa Rouhi Sarlati. 1995.

Wedding picture: Homa Rouhi and Hesam Sarlati 1945

Ladan Amouoghli (Nima's wife) with son Ryan (Homa's great grandson)

Part Two:
Memories from the Iranian Revolution

MARCH 3, 1976,

Starting today, March 3, 1976, I decided to write down a few lines about what is happening to me and to my country. I will find the opportunity to think again about what I have done, find my own self, and leave a memory from days of the revolution.

It is two months since I started my job as deputy minister at the Ministry of Industries and Mines in charge of Administrative and Parliament Affairs. I am so busy that I don't know my days from my nights. On the days when they were discussing the government budget in the Budget Committee of the Parliament, I was there until two or three in the morning, listening to the complaints of the members of Parliament that were a show of oratory. Whatever it was, the backstage show was over. In two more days, the show will be started in the open stage of the Parliament. I should expect the same scenes and stories about poverty in faraway parts of the country and the extravagance in the capital city that makes me sad. Sometimes I felt that we were at the dead end of the road and had no way to escape. As usual, at the last minute, the miracle happens and everything goes in the normal route and moves along. The budget has a deficit and income is less than the expenses. It is expected that the deficit is covered by higher oil prices.

It was interesting to see how the representatives of government agencies took advantage of their friendship with MPs. Those who were more logical and had a better relationship with MPs could easily get approval for their projects without having any problem. Those who could not make friendly relations were in trouble. During debate of the budget, two ministers were changed. Ghasem Motamedi, with fourteen years of experience at Isfahan University, was appointed as the minister of science and higher education. He had been expecting to get this job for a long time. He told me this when he was the chair of the Rastakhiz Party.

I have spoken of the Rastakhiz Party. I have to admit that without any efforts I was involved with the party. I was a member of the executive board, member of the supervisory board, and deputy of the No. 1 committee headed by Dr. Manouchehr Ganji. Due to his activities in the party, Ganji became the minister of education. He tried to fulfill the requirements of the educational staff in the shortest time possible. He progressed in some of his plans, such as establishment of a teacher's bank. In one of the meetings of the party for the 8 Esfand (February 22) anniversary of granting the right for voting to women, I stated that for further participation of women in the political life of the state, they should have equal opportunities in order to make them ready for more responsibilities.

MAY 11, 1977

When I decided to write down my memories, I could not think of having any delay in my writing. It is almost two months and ten days from my last note. Today I have time to write more. One of my childhood wishes was to write an attractive book so that one was not able to close the book before they finished it. One day I shall fulfill my desire. I had a hard life, but today I am on my own feet and have helped people in different grounds. I worked hard for women's emancipation, because I suffered for being a woman. I am happy that today I have good experience in women's studies. My interest started from the day I entered into the faculty of law and studied judicial law. I was dreaming of being a lawyer in order to defend women in the courts. My dream never materialized. I was an employee of Bank Melli Iran with ten years working experience when I received my Bachelor of Arts degree in judicial law from Tehran University. I did not have the courage to leave a good job and start a new career. I do not regret the case, however, because I was not certain about the possibility of my success.

At that time, I was introduced to Princess Ashraf Pahlavi, the head of the Iranian Women's Organization, and appointed as director general of the organization. Two years into this position, I rendered valuable services to Iranian women. I then participated as a volunteer on the board of directors until the revolution.

After being secretary general of the Women's Organization, I started my work in the Ministry of

Economy as director general of foreign trade in charge of trade with the United States and Europe. It was an interesting job, because I mostly was involved with foreigners who came to Iran for trade negotiations or went on trips for trade negotiations. I have good memories from my trips to Belgium, India, and Pakistan. The minister of economy was Hushang Ansari, who had been transferred from the job of ambassador in the United States. He was a hard-working, clever, and impatient man, and no anticipation worked for him. The atmosphere was terrifying, intimidating, and at the same time, with expectation of reward.

During Ansari's time, great changes took place in the ministry. It was expanded and many new young staff, especially those educated abroad, were attracted to the ministry. Ansari was egotistic, clever, and contemptuous. He was trying to achieve more privileges and attain a high-ranking job in the era of no trust or stability. He was very courageous and generous in spending public money.

SEPTEMBER 27, 1978

One year and five months have passed since I wrote my last note. I am ashamed of working less efficiently. During this time, some very important events happened where I was in the middle. They are valuable and memorable happenings.

In August 1971, after thirteen years, Hoveyda was removed from the position of prime minister. I have to say that the best time for the people in Iran was wasted with pretence, false statements, extravagance, and demagogy. Such days will not return to the life of the nation. Huge income from the sale of oil came to the treasury. It was gone with wind, as it came by wind.

What remained was inflation, dissatisfaction, and higher expectations from people. During Hoveyda's time, censorship, threats, and brainwashing was so widespread that even within families there was no trust and unity. People were scared of each other.

Oil money was used for unnecessary commodities, and a portion was given to foreign countries on loan, such as loan to African countries for construction of a refinery. This was when there were still people in rural areas that lived in the medieval period. Necessities of life, such as health, housing, and education, were not available to them. Wasting the oil money, the abuse of public funds, and favoritism were common practices. Although decisions were made by the prime minister, he ignored criticism and faced it with ridiculous behavior. During the thirteen-year period, censorship was so tight that media and public meetings were full of false statements. Every day, intentionally or unintentionally, the prime minister made the burden of responsibility heavier on the Shah and his family, to the extent that people assumed that every corruption was the Shah's fault.

Hoveyda was replaced by Jamshid Amuzegar, a philanthropist and clever, well-educated man with self-admiration. He did not care for others and believed that he was able to solve every problem by himself, and also solve the problems of the thirteen previous years. He attempted to give some freedom to people, which resulted from the election of Jimmy Carter as president of the United States. Carter claimed his ideal to promote human rights and pushed the other countries to give freedom to their citizens.

One year after his assignment to the position of prime minister, when he was preparing his annual report, Amuzegar was deposed from the job due to several events.

Using the narrow road to freedom, people made some demonstrations against the government, which resulted in great chaos in the provinces. Letters were distributed during dark nights and criticisms were raised. A minority of opposition had been organized in Parliament, and they started to make open complaints. Pezeshkpour, leader of the opposition, made strong complaints against the Rastakhiz party and Hoveyda government. He courageously declared that he resigned from the party that was not able to fulfill the wish of the people and was making trouble for them. The other members of Parliament followed him. The Shah had no choice but to confess that Rastakhiz was not an all-embracing party, and that people were free to participate in parties as they liked.

This was the beginning of the freedom opportunity for political activists. As a result, the political parties that were stopped in the past started their activities once again. Media used this freedom and made very bold and courageous criticisms about the government. At the same time, some people started to make demonstrations, break windows, bomb and burn, and take part in other destructive activities. The religious leaders who had been inactive and isolated became active and opened a way to freedom for dissidents. Clergies used this opportunity and gathered their supporters; they made a front against the government.

At the same time, the freedom of women was damaged badly. Liberation of women stopped and started to go backward. In a short time, uncovered women were in trouble. No opportunity was left for women.

In his last days, the Amuzegar government faced a

terrible scandal. The Cinema Rex in Abadan was set on fire and four hundred people were killed. Chaos ensued. Rumors were spread that the government could not bear the open political era and committed this scandal to have an excuse for announcing martial law and getting rid of the demonstrations.

Those who were supposed to fight against corruption were deeply involved in it. Amouzegar changed his cabinet several times. He created a web of autocracy around himself. His time was wasted on writing rules, organizing committees, and making timetable plans. He was not able to finish a single useful plan. He initiated some rules about fighting against land grabbing and the rent of vacant houses and so on; none of them worked. The same happened to the other useful laws that he had in mind. Those corrupted people had their own solutions to the new rules. If they were driven from a door, they arrived from a window. The corrupted government was in power and working.

I started my job during Hoveyda's time with Farokh Najmabadi, who was dismissed from Amouzegar's cabinet. I was appointed to the job of deputy minister in charge of Parliament and Administrative Affairs with a new minister, Mohammad Reza Amin.

When opposing activities, firing, and riots accelerated, the Shah realized that the situation could not continue. He appointed Jaffar Sharif Imamy as prime minister, who had been chairman of the senate and a trustworthy friend. Sharif Imamy selected a group of popular old friends with good reputations. Their common backgrounds were that they were known as honest people. The cabinet was not in harmony, however. There was a thirty-year age difference between members of the cabinet. How could they have understanding and work together?

Mohammad Reza Amin was among the few ministers left from Amouzegar's cabinet. He was a very highly educated person and had valuable work experiences; he was a self-made man, trustworthy, humble, a philanthropist, and a believer in the Shah. He had no weak points in his career. Whatever responsibility was entrusted to him was performed with good management skills and care. He was a decisive man and selected his team very carefully. He consulted with his team and trusted them. He never panicked; he was cool and realistic. Working with him was my best working experience.

The general people and religious leaders did not consider the change of cabinet a great change and continued their protests. The demonstration at the end of Ramadan (Aid-e Fetr) was huge and was reflected in the world media. Religious men were leading the demonstration and communists took advantage of it. The show of unity caused disappointment for the governing body, and they were worried about losing their grip. The slogans against the regime were plenty. People were preparing themselves for greater demonstrations. The government became impatient and was regretful about the granted freedom.

On September 4, martial law was declared. People did not know about martial law and gathered in Jaleh Square to face the military forces, which resulted in many hurt victims. The problem became more acute. The new cabinet needed a vote of trust and permission from Parliament. To open a safety window for the government, they declared they would directly televise statements by members of Parliament. To use this opportunity, members of Parliament started to attack the government and expressed incapacity and bad management of the government. They made an attractive show for television, and a reputation for themselves. At last, after three days, the government achieved a vote of trust. The number of those in opposition increased from four to seventeen. It was interesting to see that even those who were speaking in favor spoke against the government. Those who voted in favor of the government hoped that in a short time the fight against corruption would start.

To answer the wishes of people, the government dismissed those who were known as corrupt persons and sent them to court. Sharif Imamy was now in the process of dealing with people who had many expectations. Every day he was giving them promises. In this regard, a few hasty works were done, and the results appeared very soon. For example, the plan for independence of universities that was presented at the same time as martial law was in front of the senate. Later they realized that it had many faults. Maybe they described that plan as a relaxing medicine to stop students and start classes at the beginning of the academic year in order to make students and teachers return to classes. The problem with the universities was so complicated that it could not be solved easily. In two years time, no teacher was teaching and no student was attending class. Riots accumulated. It was said that the government could not bear the freedom environment, so this was an excuse for declaring martial law and avoiding demonstrations.

The clergies emphasized a fight against corruption that was deeply rooted in the society. Those who were expected to fight corruption were involved in corruption and could not escape it.

OCTOBER 10, 1978

Within forty-three days from Sharif Imamy's start, as it was foreseen, a mountain of problems had formed. With martial law, all public and private organizations were on strike. The government tried to ignore them in order to avoid using military forces.

Sharif Imamy gave some allowances to key organizations, such as the National Bank, Central Bank, and Telecommunication and Power and Oil Company, which caused acceleration of expectations by others that were asking for the same benefits. In the future of the government, there was no sign of relief. Mistake after mistake made the problems more acute. Dissatisfaction spread all over. Even school children went to the streets, and in a few cases faced the military and were murdered, which caused strikes in all schools.

Everybody wanted more money and did not care if that caused inflation or the situation to stay the same. The truth was that during the many years that we had income from oil, they used it mostly for purchase of arms and unnecessary factories. Public employees were not taken care of. Offices were filled with dissidents and idle people, along with some corrupted ones. We were on a no-exit road, and the future was dark. Hasty solutions would not help; using force and suffocation did not work. A country with plenty of oil income faced a deficit in the budget. The government decided to close some of the less useful public offices. The problem was so complicated that there was no time for any reform.

Oppositions came from every group: the clergy, professors, public employees, private sectors, industries, teachers, and students. There was no one to take responsibility. If the cabinet members could not understand each other, how could they understand others?

The situation was so serious that they had to find a quick solution, because continuation of their way things were almost impossible. There was no ethics, humanity, consciousness, or equity. Everybody was seeking benefit for themselves and did not have mercy on each other. They felt a sickly pleasure in hurting others. Newspapers used this feeling and wrote things that pleased those people.

Zan Rooz, a magazine that was of low standard from the viewpoint of ethics and culture, attacked Mahnaz Afkhami, the minister in charge of women affairs, and accused her of many crimes. She was dismissed from the position of minister for fifty days. When she was in power, she was flattered; now she was accused. Without having any gender prejudice, she worked for women's enhancement within the limits of her power. Then, the Women's Organization started a downward movement and changed its objectives to accord with the government.

With the spending of millions, no step was taken for educating women about their rights. In the first attempts of clergies, women covered themselves in chador (veils) and kept to their homes. They lost their managerial positions and had no hope for a bright future.

Although there is a good chance to be born a girl; no matter how much you have, you are never counted as a human being with equal rights. The people expect you to be beautiful, act like a doll, and do secondhand works.

My high position in the government is going to terminate soon. I am forty-seven years old and spent all my adult life working hard and learning as much as possible. I am satisfied and at the same time regretful with my past days. I regret that my life was full of excitement and worry about my duties, and I had no time for enjoying my family life. I am the only woman left in the position of deputy minister.

OCTOBER 22, 1978

Every day the situation is getting worse. Strikes are spread all over. The objectives are normal, but some meaningful political wishes are involved as well. The government has promised to fulfill the material request without thinking about the inflationary results.

Government works are halted; the strike is a good excuse not to do anything. Income sources from oil proceeds and taxes are diminishing. Sellers are selling their goods at any price they like, and those who need theses goods or services have no choice but to buy them. Schools are closed and universities are in political chaos. Most factories are closed and production is a big headache. Everybody expects a miracle. Newspapers have found more freedom, and they add fuel to the fire.

Today Shrif Immay was invited to a private meeting; the purpose is to make conciliation between the cabinet and Parliament, which is very unlikely. Hundreds of questions and one impeachment were in the agenda. In the cabinet, everybody goes their own way, and there is no harmony. It is a nation that has lost its way, and nobody knows what they want. Nobody can bring a wise solution. As soon as the government tries to solve a problem, another problem pops up. They expect a miracle.

I talk about miracles, because the situation is so problematic that ordinary solutions do not work. In provinces, military intervention and demonstrations happen every day. As a result, many killings are happening; the exact number is not known.

In Kerman, the riots have a different motive. Some people of the tribe called "Kouli" attacked people in the name of the Shah and set fire to mosques, libraries, and businesses, which made clergies upset. The clergies are already organized and are not willing to cooperate with the government.

Members of the National Front Party collected the remainder of their members in order to achieve power.

The Shah is not ready to give up power; he is ready to work within the constitutional law. The people around him who enjoyed privileges for many years did not want to let it go. There was a rumor about a national court for trial of those who were in power during the twenty-five years. Although some freedom is sensed, the atmosphere is still not ready for courageous actions. Everybody is wondering, and the aim of groups is not clear. Within each group, there are some philanthropists, and yet, others who oppose their ideas. This is the reason that intellectuals and humble people are not playing with their prestige in this agitated market place.

It is more than one week since Dr. Nahavandi, the minister of science and higher education, resigned. He is not willing to cooperate with this cabinet.

NOVEMBER 4, 1978

The situation gets worse every day. The country is at the height of unrest and riot. In the provinces, there is killing and obstinacy in different groups. Strikes have disabled the country. It has been about fifty days that the strikes have been going on in the Ministry of Finance, which is the vital organ of the country. The strike has gone beyond legal requests. Even elementary and high schools are now agitated like the universities.

In a week named Unity Week, university professors, students, and ordinary people were following political demonstrations. All who were on strike requested freedom of political prisoners, implementation of the constitution, and the return of Ayatollah Khomeini. The unexpected event was for the freedom of some political prisoners, which caused hot discussions. Some of these prisoners have spent thirty years in prison. By releasing those people, some of the wrongdoings and tortures of SAVAK were revealed and caused anger in the people. Newspapers reflected memories of the released prisoners, and they spoke clearly about them. It was amazing to see how they could keep people dormant and unaware for years. The small group who did find out about the crimes by authorities were tortured and silenced.

Many crimes were committed for the sake of remaining in power. Control of ideas and thoughts, closing mouths, and suffocating cries resulted in today's riots. Due to bad management, a generation of youth never experienced freedom. They were kept in prisons to be far from reality. The first breeze of freedom disclosed the terrible secrets.

If there is continuous freedom for a few years in Iran, then people may be able to balance their way of thinking. These days it is useless to expect correct behavior. It is like a bull in the arena that attacks whatever is in its way. Today's society looks like a show to expose power.

You can not speak about considering the prestige of the others and ethics. Accusation is an easy thing to do. Whoever is able to ruin a prestigious character is the winner of the race.

I wrote about freedom, but I do not believe that what we have achieved could be called freedom. There are some happy moments when the media shows and writes about what has happened. Everybody is so amazed about the list of claims by people. I am afraid that tolerance of the freedom givers is going to end very soon, and these riots will result in another dictatorship. It is unlikely that after experiencing light one can go back to darkness.

A strike in oil industries resulted in the cutting of oil exports, which is a catastrophe. As a result, we lose millions of dollars every day. In the absence of oil and gas, the daily life of people is jeopardized.

A strike by Iran Air resulted in the stoppage of our connection with other countries and provinces. People demand the Americans be expelled, which is not an easy thing to do.

Ayatollah Khomeini, leader of opposition inside and outside of Iran, is not ready to make any compromise with the Shah and the new government.

There was rumor about making a referendum to show that they do not like monarchy. Great powers, such as the United States, United Kingdom, France, and Germany, have supported the regime. With regard to the geographic location of Iran, they deemed the support in their own interests. Members of the National Front are trying hard to find a solution to solve the crisis.

Sharif Imamy shuffled the cabinet and changed two more ministers. One was Azmoun, a minister without a portfolio, and the other was Bahery, minister of Justice. The two of them were not trustworthy characters. Ghazi

Shariatpanahi replaced Nahavandi and became the minister of science and higher education. Newcomers Paydar, Najafi, and Ghazi have good reputations. Can the new ministers answer claims from the government or not? It is not clear.

At the end of every day, I ask myself: "How can I spend one more day in this situation?"

November 5, 1978

Yesterday the situation got worse. A group gathered in front the university. They were confronted with military forces. People said sixty-five were killed; the government says nobody was killed. The scene was displayed on TV. The praying taking place and religious slogans were very impressive. Suddenly, a bomb, tear gas, and "Allah Akbar" ("God Is Great") went on the air, and the TV showed the miserable appearance of Dr. Shaibani, the chancellor of Tehran University. The eighty-two-year-old man tried hard to keep the soldiers out of the university, but he did not succeed. What should not have happened did happen. I think continuation of work at the university is impossible. We wait and see.

November 16, 1978

The outcome of the riot at the university was terrible. People took to the streets and burned the city. Demonstrations and strikes maximized. Anti-government and anti-regime slogans spread all over the city without any reservation. There were many slogans written on the walls. Every bank, cinema, and liquor store was set on fire. The restless crowd moved in the city. Even the city buses that were for public use, and some of them newly purchased, were set on fire. People broke the fire extinguisher vehicles and wounded the drivers. Youths made anti-regime labels and compelled drivers to stick them to their windows. They asked them to keep their headlights on to show victory.

In 25th Shahrivar Sq. in Tehran people burned a nine-story building that was a BMW car exhibit and the National Gas Company head office. The building was burned so seriously that only a mountain of tangled iron remained of the building.

So far, the Ministry of Industries and Mines was quiet. Then suddenly, very nasty slogans were chanted under the window of the minister's room. During several terrible hours, we witnessed a demonstration from the minister's room together with other deputies. At last the city came to a halt, and people were wandering the streets to find some means to reach their homes.

It was difficult to fill the gas pumps, and as a result, all vehicles were stopped. The bus company stopped working because of heavy damage and danger for the drivers. Banks were closed. Bakeries could not bake bread due to not having fuel.

It was a horrible time for people; it was worse than war time. During war time, people safeguard their public properties. These people burned their own properties and took living facilities from themselves and their fellow citizens.

In this chaotic situation, the media increased tension through constant report of the riots. I hope such events never happen again in Iranian history. Nowadays our life is day by day. Every day I am worried about the next day. Time brings no pleasure and is full of worry.

It is sad to witness the ruin of a nation, loss of faiths, and the change of facades. It requires great courage to follow my own way, although some reasoning weakens my belief.

I am under pressure to leave my job and think about my own safety. I do not like to change my way. I do not mind about my future. I have had good days in my country and enjoyed the benefits. Today my country is sick, bankrupt, and on the verge of a great change. I do not leave it, and I will be loyal to the end.

Those who change their mind in the middle of the way are failures, not those who fight to the end and stand for their honor.

NOVEMBER 7, 1978

What happened today was expected. Sharif Imamy resigned and a martial force replaced his cabinet. In a message to the people, the Shah confessed to his mistakes. He said: "I have heard your revolution message. I hereby undertake to compensate what happened in the past." I do not comprehend the effects of such a message. What do people think who have heard such promises many times? For sure, the power of the people and their unity has been taken seriously. On the other hand, it is another show that is going to take place.

People have relaxed and accepted the martial law. In the marital cabinet, the prime minister and three ministers are from military personnel. So far there was no time for selection of ministers. Three civil ministers for Foreign Affairs, Telecommunication, and Industries and Mines were reinstated. It is possible that other ministers are selected among civilians.

Dr. Amin, the minister of Industries and Mines, is a philanthropist and inevitably wants to rescue the Shah and the country. He thinks he can get along with a military cabinet better than a civil cabinet.

Yesterday and today, the city was almost quiet; all were afraid of the soldiers. The first action was to solve the problem of shortage of food and fuel, which gradually worked. Another action that made people happy was the arrest of some government staff known to be corrupt. It was counted as a step in fulfillment of the Shah's promises.

Newspapers are on strike, and the radio and TV are silent once again. They broadcast short news without any interpretation. It would be good if they aired real news.

The great movement of religious leaders showed no reaction. Surely they are not sitting quiet, and they are planning for their own safety. Against every effort of the Shah and the government, a coalition between the National Front and religious leaders did not work.

The new government promises that it will end as soon the danger is removed, and it will submit power to a civil cabinet.

I foresee that we will have the same problems when we start moving toward freedom. If we could overcome this crisis, we could make our route to freedom shorter. Now we have returned to the beginning and must start all over again.

NOVEMBER 14, 1978

I am so sad and disappointed. The nights are more terrible than the days. We have no friendly conversation and no message to give us energy. Nights look longer with loneliness and no plan for the future. This is our life today. A city with no newspaper is like a room that has no windows; a silence that has thousands of cries. Nobody knows what is going to happen. A bitter longing is shadowed all over the country. It is hard to hide your worry in the presence of armed soldiers. When I see the armor, I think how one of those bullets is able to pierce the heart of someone. I imagine myself in the shoes of a mother who follows her child to school with fear and worry.

What happened is that we do not comprehend each other. Even mothers and children do not talk the same language. We are all isolated, and nobody is interested in taking part in the parties.

It is almost two weeks now that the army has been in power. Signs of fire are all around. Today we once again heard the roar of bullets disturb our semi-tranquility. People's resistance is not terminated. Markets, schools, and universities are closed. All together the atmosphere has changed. The strike in the oil industry has ended. There is great resistance against foreign experts.

Those who were not courageous left Iran. Those who take advantage are staying at any price.

A few cheap newspapers are published. Those long-time closed magazines are starting again. A strike by newspapers and TV is continuing. TV programs are short, and they mean nothing; they try to cover up the real stories.

People are insisting on the punishment of high-ranking officers in the government, including Hoveyda, the former prime minister, Valian, the Governor of Khorasan, Nasiri, the head of the security organization, and Nikpay Tehran, the mayor. The Justice Administration is getting ready for courts to start, but the procedure is not clear.

The other members of the cabinet are civil persons and mostly the ministers of the previous cabinet.

Parliament and the senate have a very vague position against the government. For the first time in many years, the sessions were held without having any speaker before coming into order; they do not know what to do with the martial government. Some MPs were concerned about the closure of Parliament. It seems that they have changed the unfriendly attitude they showed to Sharif Imamy. If the government is able to implement some positive plans, it is possible to receive support by Parliament and the people. So far, one member of Parliament and one senator have been arrested, and a few more are on a waiting list.

Gradually, the strike of government offices is ending. However, the situation in the Ministry of Finance and Economic Affairs is still not normal. In the Ministry of Commerce and Telecommunication, political demands prevail.

Religious leaders have lost contact with people through newspapers and TV. They are not heard anymore.

One of the most effective steps taken by the Shah was to announce that a committee will investigate the wealth of the royal family, and the way they made their wealth. They will return whatever belongs to the people. Some changes occurred to the Pahlavi Foundation.

At present, the problem is the situation of universities and reconciliation with religious leaders. It seems that none of them will reconcile easily. In case the authorities make understanding with religious leader the problem of universities will be solved as well.

Issues with the Communists, who have taken fat fish from muddy water, also remain. They issued widespread propaganda and largely distributed their books and ideology. When the situation turns to normal and the opposition is limited, they could be prevented from making trouble, unless there is a settlement between the Communists and religious leaders; that is another big problem.

NOVEMBER 21, 1978

Days pass, a few people try to calm the crowd, and many more are trying to offset their efforts. Gradually, Tehran returns to normal. After a long closure, the bazaar started its activity again. Elementary schools are open, but there is no news about the return of newspapers. Radio and television are not back to normal. There are rumors that the opposition spent money to continue the strikes. They want censorship to stop, which is impossible with martial government.

Eight more ministers have been introduced to the Parliament; they are the same people in Sharif Imamy's cabinet. There are few Military men in the cabinet. The new ministers are among well-known and unknown people. Most of the deputy ministers who are familiar with the job were also selected as ministers.

I spent four days at the Caspian in order to think about what I am doing. As from today (November 21), two consecutive days will be assigned for discussion about the program of the government. Twenty representatives will speak in favor and against the program. The scenes and presentations will be repeated.

The government program, in short, consists of bringing peace and providing requirements for the people. Nobody can protest the program, especially that the government emphasis is clearing the road for a free election. Foreign provocation about Iran's events has mounted. Foreign newspapers write long articles about the situation in Iran. Some of the riots, such as slogans and pictures from Tehran University bringing the Shah's statue down, are printed in foreign newspapers but not in Iranian papers.

Consortium negations have not reached a favorable

conclusion. It seems that until this problem is solved, the domestic problems will not be solved. Hushang Ansary, who went abroad for negotiation with consortiums, will not come back. Now, whoever can find an escape will go out of Iran. Those who are well-off can go anywhere and feel themselves at home.

Days ago when I was going north from Chalus Road, while looking at the jungles that were covered in fall colors, my heart started to beat faster. I thought, *My God, how I love this country. Whatever happens is better than going to exile.*

NOVEMBER 22, 1978

A volcano is under the peaceful appearance. Sometimes the sound of a bullet breaks the silence, but you can not say where it came from, how many were killed, and why the soldiers shoot.

It is hard to witness a catastrophe instead of betterment. As it is going on, there is no hope for any progress. Every day there is a new problem. Sources of living are getting dry.

DECEMBER 2, 1978

Today is the first day of Moharam (mourning month). Last night there were shouts of "Allah akbar" ("God is great") and the roar of bullets that kept the city awake. The city is in an unusual state. At the back of my office is the forensic office, where I can see ambulances full of bodies. Employees leave the office and go to the streets so that they do not have to pass them. The situation is getting worse every hour.

The martial government was not able to restore security, but it has clearly increased the chaos. We have no media to give us news; it is all rumors spreading quickly. People are upset because they have no electric power or telephone service, and there is a shortage of oil and gas. Nobody knows how long this will continue. It is anticipated that during the first two weeks of Moharam things will get worse.

It is so awful to live in waiting and not know what is going to happen. It is sad to think that the good old days are not coming back. The flimsy economy has fallen over our heads. The government is making people miserable by all the lies and misuse of public assets. Today they answer the unhappy people with bullets.

Last week an event caused the height of anger in the people. There was a publication of a list of employees of the Central Bank that showed the influential civil and military personnel, who were responsible for the life and belongings of the people, taking their assets outside of the country. Figures were so large that it surprised everyone. Once again the deprived people were being abused. The mental effects of the publication of such a list was so deep for those people who could not imagine such things. The names that appeared in the list were the same people that were considered by society as "corrupted people who gathered their assets through incorrect ways."

DECEMBER 3, 1978

The last demonstrations started after curfew hours. "Allahu Akbar" and "la Elah Ela Allah" ("God is great" and "No God except Allah") are heard from the rooftops in the middle of night.

Today there were three impeachments, some questions and notifications from the Parliament. Strikes and work stoppages continue in every ministry and store in the city. The future of the government and the country is not clear.

No organization will give proper news. Notices from the government are contrary to the observation of people.

Both sides, the clergy and the martial government, insist on their wishes. There is sorrow and bewilderment in the people's looks. The situation is worse than war time.

DECEMBER 4, 1978

At 9:00 PM, curfew hours start. Shouts of "Allah akbar" rise to the sky from rooftops and are followed by bullet roars that shake the walls of homes.

Most people are aimless and sad; they believe in nothing. There is no dialogue except about political matters and expressions of worry. In a war against a foreign enemy, they could bear the hardship, but today they are fighting against their own people. Whatever was built during the past years is falling down by a breeze. All that remains are ashes that a few take care.

In a system where banks and treasuries are not working, nothing remains normal. We expect a miracle. Those who are ruined are not able to reconstruct. Who is going to solve the problems? How long can we feed ourselves with leftovers? What will be the future if production is not started?

A feeling of emptiness has taken courage out of the people. Perhaps we are committing group suicide as a tribe on Goya Island.

DECEMBER 16, 1978

Tasoua and Ashoura (mourning days for Imam Hossein) were terrible. Everybody expected final days; nothing happened and the situation got more complicated. Three days prior to Ashoura a holiday was announced, which happened to be an opportunity for clergies to make up their position Due to religious beliefs, the prime minister ordered a ceasefire. The opposition took advantage and heightened the demonstrations in every city. In Tehran, two million people participated in the demonstrations, which were very populated for the first time. At the demonstration, which was held in an organized way, there were no remarks about Ashoura and Tasoua; everybody asked about the departure of the Shah. This demonstration cut the relationship between the Shah and the people. The government announced that from now on no group is allowed to make any demonstrations.

In a statement from the prime minister, he said, "I am ashamed to tell you that due to strikes, we do not have any oil for export or for internal consumption, and we should import oil from other countries."

A power cut is continued every night from 9:00 PM to 12:00 PM. There is a long cue in front of oil stores. A miserable winter is coming. Every day there are rumors of the Shah's departure and the start of a monarchy committee, which is denied by media.

Soldiers are scattered; a few of them have left the garrisons. Negotiations with the National Front did not work; they do not like to take part in the cabinet. General Azhari, the prime minister, announced that the government employees will not receive their salaries if they continue their strike, and they will also be expelled. Now the people are talking from an upper-hand position and the government from a weak position.

If Government employees stop working in protest to the Prime Minster's statement, can the Government expel them all? The prime minister told them, "Please go back to work, otherwise we shall have no money to pay your salary, and the subsidies will not continue." The opposition wants to disable the government. It seems they were successful.

Parliament protested the government. There is no real news from the mass murder in the cities. Iran has attracted the attention of the world. Oil negotiations of OPEC and the Oil Consortium are going on. Before, Iran had a positive stand, but now is in a weak position. Those who are parties to the negotiations could turn the atmosphere in their favor because Iran is in a weak position and does not have the support of Parliament or the people.

To make the clergy happy, they try to annul the laws that conflict with Islam. The first victims were women. To make the religious people happy, they are ready to let the fifteen-year-old girls get married. They forbid social work for women, made abortion illegal, and allowed for polygamy for men.

In a short time, we turned back fifty years. Whatever was given to women was abolished quickly. If we have made sacrifices to gain such rights, perhaps we should not let go so easily. The future is dark and unknown for women.

The economic situation is so entangled that there is no hope for the future. Even if the Shah is gone, there is nobody to take care of such a situation. It is possible that after the riots, there will be dictatorship and suffocation. To be realistic and to consider the events, I foresee that the future will fall at the hands of those who will govern by force and rely on arms.

It seems that there is no return for the Shah. In the long years of monarchy, the unwise government and corrupted relatives closed every door. Today people cannot forget what has happened to them. If there was a wise government in power, we would not have such a great population in poverty, with people who do not have the primary tools for living.

The cruel Security Organization has evacuated the country from capable and worthy people. That is the reason that there is no hand extended to help the regime. They have marked people and sent them away from the system. Now, whoever has cooperated with the government during the eleven years is guilty. Who is able to restart production? Inexperienced youth or disabled old people? I soothe myself by remembering that this country has had hardships throughout history and always survived. Maybe this time we will be saved as well. But this time it is not a joke; it is for the price of fifty years of backwardness.

DECEMBER 19, 1978

Yesterday Ayatollah Khomeini announced a National Mourning Day and holiday. Closings are not happening all over; schools and some shops are open, and the situation is normal. Now, however, everybody is suffering from a shortage of oil. It is a cold winter, and people are used to overconsumption of oil for heat and light. It now takes hours to stand in the queue for oil. The strike of the oil employees is over, but there is no improvement in the situation. The power is cut nightly; no TV and radio makes our life miserable.

Today the BBC claimed that there was a riot in Tabriz Garrison; this was denied by the national radio. OPEC increased oil prices 10 percent for the coming year. This has made our Western friends unhappy, and they are complaining about oil prices going up in their countries.

Foreign countries are trying to intervene in Iran. But they know if one country is doing so, the others will do so as well. The situation in Iran is important to the world. They know that if the stability of Iran is endangered, it will affect the political balance of the world.

We are told that the strike of oil employees is over, but the power cut at night is hard to bear. Today it was said that a non-martial government will come to power. It is possible that Dr. Sadighi, a well-known and moderate man, will come to power. The martial government made remarkable mistakes during his time which disappointed everyone. It is impossible to hope that a government will come to power which existing groups are not supporting.

Today marks two years that I have been working in the Ministry of Industries and Mines; two years with new experiences and some good and bad memories. How hopeful I was when I started this job; how hopeless I am now, and how dark my future is. Every day I expect some new events. Nobody knows what the future will be. It is possible that one of these days my career will be over. It will be great if I manage to finish it in a peaceful manner.

People have no mercy; you cannot trust your close friends. My most valuable gain was the wide recognition of people, and the opportunity to talk with them. I wish I could be of service to my people. I am not worried about my own life, but about my country. I feel so sad when I see my country being ruined.

Yesterday the schools were opened after six months, but the students were sent back to their homes. In no other country are people wasting their mental and material assets as they do here. Why isn't politics practiced in elementary schools? Who is going to come to power who thinks that it is good to have an illiterate and unaware younger generation?

The political problem is not solved thus far. General Azhari, the militant prime minister, has suffered a heart attack due to hard work and pressure and was hospitalized. The strike and darkness are continuing. Everybody is in a state of wilderness and expects a greater disaster. They all ask for the Shah's departure, but nobody knows what will happen then. It seems that this is a common request for all strikers, rioters, and even students Fighting against corruption is everybody's desire, if it happens, it may bring peace. The volume of corruption and those who were involved is so vast that there seems to be no solution to the problem.

DECEMBER 30, 1978

The most terrible days in the history of the country have happened. It has been two days since provision of oil and gas has stopped. As a result, the fineries are stopped, and all the activities are halted; even the purchase of bread is not possible.

If Dr. Sadighi agreed to become the prime minister, people would be happy and the hard situation would ease. However, he did not accept the offer because the opposition groups would not cooperate. Yesterday it was thought that Shapour Bakhtiar would be the prime minister. Immediately again, the party members announced that they would not support him.

The cold weather and the shortage of fuel in the beginning of the winter have made the people upset and unhappy.

Last Wednesday, there was a very serious contact between employees of the Ministry of Industry and Mines and the soldiers of the royal guard who were stationed in the ministry. It was possible that they opened fire on people who were chanting slogans against the Shah. As I was in charge at the ministry, I interfered and asked the revolutionary staff to stop their chanting so that the shooting would stop. The incident was somehow stopped, but it was not the end. Clergies have decided to make a great demonstration to show their sympathy to families of those who were murdered in recent days.

Due to the gas shortage, many could not attend the demonstration, but those who were present were enough to make trouble. There is hate among the soldiers and people. Armed forces dare to shoot. At night, the roar of bullets breaks the silence.

Now it is clear that the military government can do nothing, and the problem is getting more complicated. Even within families, there are political discussions going on.

At my work, the danger has become serious. Unknown telephone calls and the spread of lies threaten those who remain in their jobs. Most of these people are not happy about their situation.

The radical revolutionary people became tired. They are hoping for whatever can happen in order for their lives to go back to normal. Iranian radio and TV seems like it is broadcasting from another world. They spread the foreign news in detail and repeat the stories and songs of old days. Just recently they spoke about the effects of gas shortage.

DECEMBER 31, 1978

When the news about the appointment of Shapour Bakhtiar to the position of prime minister spread by foreign broadcasts, the Iranian radio announced the event and stated that he would start his work when Parliament gave him a vote of trust. Much hardship is already foreseen for him. The radio stated that Bakhtiar told them that, the "Shah promised to go for treatment out of the country in proper time."

Last night we were told that the royal family had gone to the United States. This shows that staying in Iran is not safe for them anymore.

Dr. Karim Sanjabi, leader of the National Front Party, announced the party's disagreement with Shapour Bakhtiar being made prime minister. Like Ayatollah Khomeini in Paris, they want a departure of the Shah from Iran.

Some bonus is given to the oil company staff to end their strike. They hate Hushang Ansari but respect Entezam, his replacement. Military personnel left the oil company. Some workers who were dismissed from service were called back and their homes were restored to them. They were promised a piece of the nationalized lands. Up to this date, there is no sign of an end to the strikes.

Only a few employees came to work today. Nightly darkness and bullet firing continues. Problems are so acute that there is no hope of a solution. Iran's development was as fast as its decline. The speed of decline is so fast that nothing can stop it. Maybe we should start from zero like a poor country. It is so sad to see people who had great sources of oil now in line for a few liters of oil.

People have witnessed discrimination and their

rights being demolished. Where were the people a few months ago who are shouting now? Why were they in silence? Now a big force has been established, and it is hard to satisfy them.

At last, the military government has resigned. One of the vice presidents is in charge until the vote of trust to Shapour Bakhtiar is given by Parliament. Bakhtiar spoke very humbly from the radio, which pleased everyone because he was honest. A man that suffered thirty years imprisonment for his ideas and always protested the Shah and his regime is the lost hope of the nation. Sanjanbi, from the National Front, and Ayatollah Khomeini did not support him. In his speech, Bakhtiar mentioned the Shah's departure, which did not please the opposition. They wanted an end to the constitutional regime. The Shah likes to say that when he empowered his biggest enemy and accepted his conditions, he would not be powerful even if he remained in the country.

It is possible that Shapour Bakhtiar's solution is a social democratic government. The opposition did not give him this opportunity.

We do not know about the members of the cabinet. If Bakhtiar can attract some well-reputed people to cooperate with him, the possibility of his success will increase. We can not expect the cabinet to be totally from the National Front; he should invite some members from the opposition.

The problem of gas for internal consumption is still not solved. People are waiting in long lines for gas, and they are very angry and disappointed. They expect a miracle to happen.

In Mashad, the most wild and cruel incident happened that has never happened before. People were watching the case from TV. All human values were ignored. They crucified people without any defense and court hearing. They were condemning all who cooperated with the regime; they burned their homes and did not show any mercy to those people.

JANUARY 6, 1979

I receive many calls now recommending that I leave Tehran. This is the result of thirty years of service to the country, and now I have to escape the many accusations. I finally went to Sari to reduce my anxiety.

A royal order for Prime Minister Shaour Bakhtiar was issued, and he started to select his cabinet. There is a rumor that the military commander of Tehran, General Ovaisi, has run away. It is possible that people may relax because of his departure. He was known to be very cruel. People are happy that he ran away. Maybe he is going away because he provided facilities for the Shah's trip. People think that the Shah will go away for a short time. In two days, the cabinet will be introduced to Parliament.

It is said that Abbasgholi Bakhtiar, ex-deputy minister of the Ministry of Industries and Mines, will be the minister. If he is the minister, I will have no problem. My return to Tehran depends on having gas for the trip.

It is two days since the situation has improved, but all activities are stopped. The railroads, airlines, banks, and oil industries are all on strike. The restart of activities depends on the end of the strike in the oil industry.

Two people from the National Front, Mehdi Bazargan and Habibi, along with a group of clergies went to Abadan to convince the employees to start their work, at least for internal consumption. It seems that they did not succeed.

Bakhtiar announced the plan for his cabinet, the same that people desired, including: a serious fight against corruption, dissolution of the SAVAK Security Organization, freedom of the press and parties, and stoppage of the sale of oil to Israel and South Africa. Bakhtiar asked for some time for those actions in case he does not succeed in changing their views.

The big problem is the disagreement of Ayatollah Khomeini with the temporary departure of the Shah. He wants the removal of the constitutional government and the start of an Islamic republic. People are having a hard time; they cannot trust promises.

We hear no word about current problems from the media. Only Tooraj Frazmand, the director general of radio and TV, makes political comments once in a while.

JANUARY 7, 1979

Forty-four years ago on this day, Iranian woman were freed from their veils by Reza Shah, and they stepped into enhancement and progressed quickly. There were times when being a woman was a privilege, but today it is a weak point and a good reason for being laid off. I remember the Women's Congress where they exaggerated the power of women, which ended in the selection of a woman, Mahnaz Afkhami, as the minister in charge of women's affairs.

I introduced myself to the new minister of Industries and Mines, Abbasgholi Bakhtiar. I told him not to worry about the appointment of new vice-ministers. He told me it is a very crucial time, and we should all sacrifice for the freedom of our country.

Working in such conditions and under such pressure

is very hard. My family and friends insist that I quit my job. But I do not want to quit in this situation.

After two months, the press started to publish again. They wrote whatever they wanted without being censored and compensated for the days they were silent. Street demonstrations continue. Clergies, under the leadership of Ayatollah Khomeini, and minority of Parliament and some well known members of the National Front party expressed their disagreement with Bakhtiar. The ministries are closed for common mourning and their closure may continue. The strike in the oil industries is over, but long oil queues are still there. Owners are afraid to open their shops and fear the crowds if they bring oil into the shop. With mountains of problems in front of this government, its success would be a miracle.

JANUARY 9, 1979

Today, the first snow of winter sat on the ground. With the public strike and lack of oil, it is a difficult time. A new problem occurred. A list of members of SAVAK has spread throughout the city. How can you speak logic to these people? This was a baseless action that everybody realized was not accurate. Clergies and parties asked people to avoid personal revenge and to stop killing people and burning their homes. A few incidents happened that caused shame for society. They did not allow people to defend themselves and condemned and punished them right away.

From the pressure of relatives and friends, I left my home and passed my days and nights in different places - those were the saddest days of my life. Those who knew me were sorry for me, and those who did not know me attributed my progress to doubtful relations.

The situation did not improve. In provinces, bloodshed and demonstrations continue. In some cities, they announce self autonomy. Some religious courts started working outside of the judicial system and did not give a chance to anybody to tell the truth. Between members of the National Front that have absolute power, there is some disagreement. Unease is high. Unemployment and poverty worries everyone. The future is doubtful and dark. Shah has not left the country and is waiting for a vote of trust for Bakhtiar. It is decided that a Monarchy Council is held - what will happen is not clear. The Clergies would like the Shah to leave forever. The Prime Minister wants the regime to stay constitutional. There are rumors about a coup d'état, but it is not known by whom. A few army generals have retired. American Generals came to Iran to help the army.

JANUARY 13, 1979

I went to the ministry after three days. It was cold and filled with worry and fear. Today was the reopening of the universities. Wherever a group of people get together, a riot happens. They do not open universities for the sake of learning. They just want a place for getting together. This is the reason that leaders of the National Front and some clergies made statements in this regard. It is not possible that the universities reopen soon.

The walls are covered with the most vulgar slogans. Every night they are covering them with some slogans against the Shah. The press prints whatever they receive, hoping for freedom. The Toudeh Party gains the most advantage from the press and gatherings.

It was promised that a power cut will not happen for a few days. However, the power line was cut from 10:00 AM today. Heavy snow covered the city. Worry and fear is everywhere. So far there is no shortage of food from the strike in the ports that stopped ships and trucks at the border; however, very soon a shortage will happen.

I have not forgotten the promises given by the ex-government. As soon as they achieved the power, they did not fulfill any of the promises. Problems are there, and the world is surprised. They all try not to interfere; maybe a solution happens automatically. Foreigners, army generals, police, gendarmerie, and the government authorities are in danger of being arrested or killed. Against recommendations of the authorities, personal revenge and hasty and illegal decision making is not finished. The Shah conditioned his departure to stability of the government, which delays it constantly. People do not accept the government and the Parliament and would like to have an Islamic republic, but it is not clear how it is going to start.

JANUARY 14, 1979

Today the plan of Dr. Shapur Bakhtiar was discussed in Parliament. As it took a long time, Parliament became agitated; everybody had some critique. How can a government that is not supported by the National Front, clergies, and people work? They are all of the opinion that if Ayatollah is not in support, the government cannot work.

Maybe there is a hidden conspiracy for sending the Shah away and bringing Khomeini in. With the crowd that demonstrated in support of Khomeini in the streets of Tehran, surely the day he comes to Iran and people see him in power, the number of supporters will be multiplied, and no government will be able to do anything against their will.

Today I have decided that I cannot mix with any of these groups. Now I give myself some time to watch the events.

Universities are starting to open for the gathering of people. Dictatorship is continuing in another form. In my view, the real philanthropists are silent and far; there are no able and wise persons to save the country. The minister of Industries and Mines, Abbasgholi Bakhtiar, is not acceptable to Parliament because of his working with Alikhani and Hushang Ansari. They have decided to reject him in a gathering of employees. A strike and severe cold cause the absence of employees.

Today there was a big demonstration in favor of Khomeini. The slogan was: "Khomeini is our leader, army is our brother." Soldiers were watching and put the flowers that were given to them on their guns.

JANUARY 16, 1979

At last, after a vote of trust by Parliament to Bakhtiar, the Shah left the country, what everyone expected happened. At 2:00 PM, celebration in the streets started. People were dancing and congratulating each other; cars had their lights on and were blowing their horns. Newspapers announced the news with the largest available print and deleted every mention of the Shah. BBC Radio said that the Shah was crying while leaving his country and went to Egypt as guest of Anvarsadat, who enjoyed the generosity of the Shah when in power.

It is said that on the fortieth day of Moharam, Khomeini will come to Iran. So far five aircraft are available to him. Some Iranian students, members of the confederation that were not allowed to come to Iran, will accompany Ayatollah.

After the departure of the Shah and the riots that are going on, it is very hard to govern, unless the nonreligious groups support Bakhtiar. If the army is not under control of the government, more soldiers will join the Khomeini camp. In some announcements, fighting against the government, Parliament, and the royal council are mentioned. It is said that Ayatollah will appoint a revolution council and a temporary government.

JANUARY 17, 1979

Last night there were demonstrations until midnight, and people toppled every statue in the city. They toppled the statue in front of Parliament. The name of Shah Mosque, which was named from Naseraldinshah's time and had nothing to do with the Shah, is now changed to Khomeini Mosque. The name of every street or place that was related to the Pahlavi dynasty is changed to Khomeini. It is sad to see ugly slogans, even with notifications by religious leaders. It seems that we need a cultural revolution before any other revolution.

History is repeating itself. Power brings prejudice, corruption, and abuse. If one person decides for a nation, it can not be absolute. If people have no chance to speak, what is the difference between a republic and constitution? If people do not respect each other's ideas and personalities, it is not important if an egg is ten or thirty tomans a kilo. When there is no security in the workplace or at your home, what is the use of money? If you have no right of choice, it does not matter whether you are under veil or not.

The prime minister is speaking about a democratic

society and blames prejudice. He does not show any weakness. The first day of Bakhtiar's official work started. If there is no hidden agreement, he shall have a hard time in front of Ayatollah. His friends in the National Front joined the opposition that have majority.

JANUARY 19, 1979

Today is fortieth day of Moharam. Great demonstrations, like Ashura and Tasoua, are going on. Today the situation has changed a lot, and the clergies have gained great success. There is a great demonstration with more than two million people, but there is also some sign of difference between the groups. The main goal, which was the departure of the Shah, has happened. Partisans of Khomeini did not let Marxists carry their banners, and they separated their line from them. Western leaders are worried about the situation in Iran. President Carter sent a message to Khomeini and asked him to give an opportunity to Bakhtiar. Khomeini answered that it has nothing to do with the West and they better not interfere with Iran's internal affairs.

MPs started to resign in case the increasing number in Parliament is dissolved. It is not clear what would happen to the country with an illegal government and a dissolved Parliament.

The head of the royal council made a visit with Khomeini. If there is more pressure it is possible that the head of the royal council and other members will resign too.

On Sunday, the prime minister said that the employees who do not return to work will not be paid. How far he can go is not clear. Today it is foreseen that there will be a contact between the soldiers and left wing people. If it happens, it would be very difficult. Religious leaders invited people to have a peaceful attitude and to not carry their own banners; this means that the movement belongs to all groups. The army general asked people to stop using slogans against the constitution. The slogan of "Islamic Republic" is against the constitution that recognized the monarchy as legal.

Every ministry is protected by the government, because they are afraid that people may occupy them. Last night it was said that Reza Pahlavi (the Shah's son) said that if people wanted him, he was ready to come back. He is in training in the United States and under twenty years of age.

JANUARY 21, 1979

Cities and roads have no security. In Ahvaz and Dezful, soldiers opened fire toward people and killed and wounded a few.

In the ministries, strikes are going on, but it is arranged that customs releases the food needed for people. The situation with oil and gasoline has not changed. Every day we have hours of a power cut. Long distance calls and connections with foreign countries are impossible. Those students who are living abroad are worried about what is happening in Iran. They have no means of returning home.

The prime minister said, "If I do not succeed, there will be a coup d'état by the army." This is what we expect every day. A few MPs have resigned. The opposition does not accept the compromises of the royal council, Parliament, and cabinet.

Ayatollah Khomeini changed his mind about coming to Iran on the fortieth day of Moharam. He will come on Friday. We are not sure if the army will bear his orders or not.

Today I saw the statue in Mokhberoldouleh Square hanging in the middle of the air. It is one week since the new minister disappeared; he did not say where he was going or who is responsible for his ministry. Today all pictures of the Shah were collected, as to avoid their burning.

JANUARY 22, 1979

Every day the situation becomes more complicated. The prime minister and the army are standing firm. Bakhtiar said that he will not give up the situation that has been given to him by the constitution. The head of royal council has resigned.

On Friday, Ayatollah Khomeini will come to Iran. A big welcome has been planned for him. Plenty of carpets are being gathered to be spread at his feet. He has decided to start a temporary cabinet and a revolution council. We have to wait and see the confrontation of the two groups, one group the people and one group the army. A solution may be that the Bakhtiar government stays in power until it is settled by referendum, and then the government will do whatever the people want. This would be the better solution. In the case that such an opportunity is not granted, there will be a coup d'état which will result in more killing and new suffocation.

Nobody knows what an Islamic republic is. They say several times that women are free; at the same time they say Muslim woman need a veil. This means that a woman without a veil is not Muslim and is subject to disrespect.

The frightening atmosphere is heavier than ever. Cities and roads are not safe. Every day there are new events, and recently it has reached the highest level. We expect to have some release in the coming week. The strikes on the people's welfare are reduced. It seems that the government is only for giving salaries and has no responsibility towards people.

This is a very sad time; there are no smiles on faces. In the gatherings of families, there are conflicts of ideas which cause silence in order to avoid discussion.

We spend our days idle with the hope of some improvement. It is almost four months since the situation has been like this. In the beginning, we thought it would be a short incident.

JANUARY 24, 1979

It was arranged that an airplane would go to Paris and bring Ayatollah Khomeini to Iran. They call this a "Revolution Flight." Suddenly everything has changed. They said that due to the strike at Mehrabad Airport, the airfield would be closed for three days. The flights were cancelled, which caused a fury with the opposition. Surely they will seek revenge.

Ayatollah Khomeini declared that when he got back to Iran, we would establish a temporary government and revolution council and announce the country an Islamic republic. Then he said, "It is not a proper time for that."

MPs said that they are standing for the constitution and do not want to dissolve Parliament. They submitted a bill regarding dissolution of SAVAK. Today a letter from Shapur Bakhtiar addressed to Khomeini was published, asking him that every action for change in the government goes through legal channels. He said he would delay his arrival to Tehran until the situation is fit for his coming. In the letter, he was humble and respectful to Khomeini. That means that if his advice is not heard, whatever happens will be the responsibility of

Khomeini. Foreign radios announced today an attempt on Khomeini's life.

Now political groups are going their own ways after fulfilling their common goal of the Shah's overthrow. Foreign radios announced that forty people and Radio Iran said one hundred people made a demonstration and called themselves supporters of the constitution.

They said that we do not want the Shah or Khomeini and supported Bakhtiar. They had some contacts with supporters of Ayatollah Khomeini. Today the United States gave some oil and gasoline to Iran for use by the army and government. At the same time, an oil well erupted in the Persian Gulf.

JANUARY 27, 1979

Due to the closure of the airport and the impossibility of the arrival of Khomeini, a bloody demonstration was made by his supporters; ten people were killed and a few were wounded. Bakhtiar suggested that Khomeini changed his mind about the formation of a revolutionary council.

At the same time, the Shah decided not to go to the United States and stay in Egypt. Some embassies outside of Iran are now taken over by supporters of Khomeini. Some students that were against the Shah and his regime came back to Iran. There was a terrible incident between demonstrators and the soldiers; at least thirty people were killed and four hundred were wounded. Mehrabad is occupied by army now. Ayatollah said that he will not accept Shapur Bakhtiar as the prime minister.

With the involvement of the people, peaceful negotiations are not possible. A number of ordinary people are carrying arms. First, a political terrorist act occurred. An MP named Daneshi was attacked and killed on his way to Parliament. The number of people murdered and wounded is filling the capacity of the hospitals. Due to demonstrations, there are not enough supplies in the drugstores. People collect equipment through donations they are collecting from households.

JANUARY 28, 1979

It seems that the army has taken over, and they agreed with sending Bakhtiar to Paris. It is not clear whether the army will tolerate Khomeini's presence and the toppling of the Shah.

Some of the personnel of the air force have shown disloyalty to the army. It is said that some of them have been executed. The situation is so confusing that nothing can be foreseen for the future. Strikes that were reduced are now increased again because of yesterday's murder. It was decided that the banks would work two days a week. It has been more than one week that they have been closed. People want their salary. Those who encourage strikes ask for their salaries at the same time. Due to not having any security, they are not ready to wait one more day because they do not know what will happen after. At present, we are sloping downhill. In case Ayatollah Khomeini does not meet with Bakhtiar, there is no chance of success and cooperation.

JANUARY 30, 1979

Our days are wasted; nobody works; every day there are demonstrations in the streets. If the economic situation starts to move at all, it will be a miracle. We hope for a miracle.

Today the airport is open, and it is said that

Ayatollah Khomeini and his companions are responsible for their own lives. It seems that the government has declared no responsibility. If a welcome is shown by a demonstration, there will be a big chaos, unless they avoid the welcome ceremony. Still, every day a few people are killed. Yesterday there were big firings in the banks, the liquor stores, Ghaleh (a special neighborhood for prostitutes), and the beer factory. Another officer was killed. Bakhtiar is trying to show himself as a powerful man, but how can he stay in power without having the support of government employees?

FEBRUARY1, 1979

At 9:30 AM, Ayatollah Khomeini arrived by Air France at Mehrabad Airport and was welcomed with glory. As he wished, his security was left to the hands of fifty thousand of supporters. It was planned that he would speak at Tehran University, but heavy crowds did not let him, and he went to Behesht Zahra (a cemetery). Again, it was planned that the ceremony would be on TV, but some problems happened, and only a few minutes of his picture were shown and then the voice was cut. This caused fury among the people. In some cities, people have broken their TV sets. From the beginning it was clear that there would be no compromise. He said that strikes will continue until a temporary government is introduced. In the beginning of the broadcast, an old song ("Marz Por Gohr") replaced the formal song of royalty.

The corruption in broadcasting Khomeini's speech was done by a group of lefties, who did so against their promise and caused great damage for the prestige of the director general of the organization and reduced the possibility of reconciliation.

Garbage was removed from streets of Tehran by the youth, as it was made ready for the welcome ceremony. As Khomeini had requested, no ornament was placed in the streets except for cars that had their lights on and were blowing their horns.

The position of the leftists is doubtful. They were cooperating with the toppling of the Shah, but the declaration of an Islamic Republic of Iran is a great danger for them.

FEBRUARY 3, 1979

I have decided not to go to work. The atmosphere is full of terror, and responding to people that have no sense of responsibility is a great burden which can only be borne when you have a philanthropist boss. It has been one month since Dr. Amin left the ministry. I knew it would be hard to continue without him, and I have now lost my faith. I knew that nobody would be a good replacement for him. Working with an incompetent government, is like welcoming danger.

It is thirty-four years from the day I started my work in Bank Melli Iran at the age of eighteen. With all of the times I have had heavy responsibility and worked with honesty, I feel that I have fulfilled my duty toward my people and my country. Today my career is terminated, and I am happy that I have done nothing wrong. I will not start any job unless the situation is better. I shall learn to use my own time and spend it as I please. These days we have no options; you may not visit those you like, and you can not go on a trip abroad. You cannot move in the streets freely, and they do not pay your salary. It is like a prison.

Today I visited Dr. Ganji, the ex-minister of education. He lives in his house without his wife and children and is expecting to leave the country and go back to his old job in the United Nations. Dr. Ganji revealed to me the secret of spreading the list of people who worked with SAVAK. He said, "When I was in power, I had the chance to speak to the Shah and asked him to do something about political prisoners and to let the International Red Cross visit the prisons and report to the world." The Shah gave permission, and the first report was terrible. SAVAK panicked and started to replace the prisoners, which was not hidden from the International Red Cross. They insisted on stopping the torture of political prisoners. The first prisoner that was released from the prison revealed the tortures by SAVAK. SAVAK realized that Dr. Ganji was involved in bringing those people to Iran. To ruin his reputation, they did different things, including starting rumors of sending money abroad by different people and creating a list of his friends that were said to be agents of SAVAK. The rumors of sending money abroad were rejected after an investigation by the Justice Administration. The list of SAVAK agents was seen as doubtful by people, because most of them were well known. Different authorities stressed that the list was not true.

FEBRUARY 6, 1979

In the first interview with internal and external journalists, Ayatollah Khomeini spoke about the formation of a temporary government and the resignation of Shapur Bakhtiar, the prime minister. A journalist asked Ayatollah Khomeini, "What is your feeling now that you are going back to your country after fifteen years?" He replied, "Nothing." This response offended people and supporters. Everybody is worried about another self-centered government in Iran.

Bakhtiar announced that, "Whoever stimulates people to internal war will be executed. If a temporary government is introduced they will be detained instantly. Some negotiations are going on between me and Ayatollah Khomeini that were denied by him."

After the arrival of Ayatollah Khomeini, the situation is more peaceful. They speak about freedom. We can say that people are more at ease. It is decided that the banks will work every other day, and there are some limitations about the withdrawal of deposits. Nikpay, the mayor of Tehran, resigned to Ayatollah Khomeini and said he is ready to be his mayor. Nikpay was immediately arrested due to having a corruption record.

Two other authorities, Majidi, the head of the Planning Organization, and Nahavandi, the director of Shahbanou Farah's office, were arrested according to article five of martial law.

The Justice Administration, due to weakness in the system and the good relationships of the accused with the judges, do not investigate their crimes.

Ardeshir Zahedi, the ambassador in the United States, was removed from his position. Still, he seems himself as an ambassador. Agreements with the United States for the purchase of arms around one billion dollars is about to be cancelled.

Students in England are going to be expelled because of not receiving money. The UK government helped them from public funds for six weeks. Students in the US universities who could not register will be expelled from the country. Due to the strikes of airlines and banks, some people are wandering in foreign countries. These are people that were envied for their extravagance.

In the Tehran market, food, fruits, and vegetables are much better. The lines for gas are getting shorter, and as a result, traffic is becoming heavier. Since there is no worry about getting tickets, the traffic is terrible.

FEBRUARY 7, 1979

Yesterday, the prime minister of revolution was introduced in a TV interview by Ayatollah Khomeini. Bazargan, the man who played a very important role in the restart of the oil industry and mediation with the opposition, was introduced as the prime minister. Bakhtiar announced that, "One country requires one government. If it is a shadow cabinet and does not proceed on severe actions I shall have no objection."

Negotiations are going on between the army authorities and the government. There is a concern about the role of the army. In case they do not tolerate the second cabinet, there is the possibility of bloodshed and internal fighting. It is possible that some high-ranking officers have changed their positions and cut their relations with the Shah and the constitutional regime.

On February 6, Ali Asghar Haj Seyed Javadi, a very decent journalist, was arrested by the military for writing an article asking the army, "You are you defending what cause?"

There are no more demonstrations in the streets; shops are open and some schools started their work. Tehran Radio, after a few days of revolutionary statements, is on strike again and mute.

Every day there is some mourning; sadness is spread over the city. The economic situation is not satisfactory. People are wandering. Employees are not sure if they will receive their salaries. Dr. Bakhtiar said, "It is impossible to give a salary to those who did not work." If the monthly salary is delayed for two days, the salary receiver's life will be paralyzed. There remains twelve days to the end of month, and then we will see who has bluffed.

There are plenty of books and newspapers available in the booths. I was worried about how can I fill my hours, but now I am reading all the time. It is a break from working and it is renewing my knowledge. It is also good for making better decisions.

I always avoided politics. Maybe it was because I did not have enough courage to handle it or I was born humble and obedient. Now everything is changed. Politics is mixed with our daily life, and we cannot be indifferent to it. We should make our choice. Not being with one group means you are with the other group; there is no being impartial. Even being silent is somehow interpreted. In a gathering of friends, you have to make your political situation clear; otherwise you will be accused of possessing a school of thought that you do not like.

Spring is on the way, and certainly the results of Iran's political spring will be shown very soon.

FEBRUARY 11, 1979

Some ministries declared agreement with the temporary government. Ayatollah Khomeini recommended the continuation of strikes to disable Bakhtiar's government. Two main newspapers, *Kayhan* and *Etelaat,* are supporting the temporary government. They printed a picture with thousands of army personnel paying respect to Khomeini. Bakhtiar said this is a montage picture. The truth is that the army personnel are divided. Some air force personnel have divided arms among ordinary people. As a result, a very severe conflict has been caused among parties, and a great number were killed.

People made protests on the roofs, burned tires, and created road blocks, making it difficult for the disciplinary forces. Military forces have reduced the people's curfew hour to start at 4:30 PM. However, people did not obey the orders and were present in the streets, which resulted in the annulment of the order.

The left wing is making more trouble with the arms they obtained and formally declaring their existence. They have accepted the leadership of Ayatollah Khomeini, and they are organizing their troops. They hope that they can replace him in a short time. Due to the popularity of Ayatollah Khomeini, people do not show any disagreement.

There is no reasonable answer to the question of: what is this Islamic republic? What worries the intellectuals is that they believe in democracy and the participation of people in the government. Today the clergies like to have absolute power for the religious leader that is called Velayat Faghih. This leader is supposed to control people and decide for them.

In the Islamic movement, a group of women appeared with hijab and full cover of the body, even hands, and practically recommended hijab for women. Separation of men and women is observed in all gatherings. Ayatollah Khomeini referred to jihad and armed fighting against the government. He worked hard on weakening the morals of army personnel and encouraged disobedience of their commanders. It was asked: "What is the meaning of jihad between Muslims?" He said, "Whoever opposes Bazargan, that is my prime minister, is an infidel."

It was decided to make a referendum about the type of government. It seems that in this chaos there is no possibility of a free election, and people are not able to express their views.

Army personnel returned to their bases. Tehran is totally at the disposal of people who are fighting with each other. Philanthropists that are not armed are hidden in their homes and do not share in this unequal fight.

There is no clear message in the program of the Bazargan government, except for handling the government and performing a referendum. This is the same Bazargan who caused the failure of Dr. Mosaddegh with his conservative decisions and did not show any courage in his works.

FEBRUARY 12, 1979

At 4:45 PM, the radio suddenly cut its program and announced that, "This is the voice of revolution, the true voice of Iranian people." They then broadcasted national songs and very provocative messages and asked the employees of radio and TV to go back to their jobs. The speakers appeared on TV with tired faces and without any make-up. They played films showing the army leaving the radio and TV buildings. From the very first messages, it appeared that Mojahedin Khalgh and the left wing have the upper hand.

Gradually, the news about the fall of government offices was on the air. The high council of the army announced his impartiality and the return of soldiers to their bases.

In Tehran, the storage of arms was set on fire, and the city was covered with smoke. TV announced that there are rumors about poisoning of the city water, which was denied by responsible authorities.

With the fall of the army bases, the arms fall in the

hands of the people. Several notices were issued by the revolution leaders regarding the misuse of the arms.

Army commanders announced their cooperation with the revolution. Jamshidieh Garrison, the prison for leaders of the old regime, was set on fire. People were worried about the escape of the prisoners.

The TV broadcast different notices. It was said that Nikpay, the former Tehran mayor, and Rahimi, the army commander, are being detained by people. So far the revolutionary forces are not in power. Saltanatabad Garrison is surrounded by the royal guard. They asked for help.

Many governors and ambassadors are yielding to the new forces.

Last night, the TV was broadcasting the notices; then the radio started to do so. They were asking people to stop killing and firing. It was difficult to preach to those who were armed and had no conscious.

As of last night, there is more talk about the left wing, and not about Ayatollah Khomeini. It seems that they have taken leadership in the name of religion.

FEBRUARY 13, 1979

I returned to Tehran after five days and was terrified to see that every young man has a pistol. Pits remain in the streets that were dug by people fighting with the armed forces. It is a real fight scene. Although the army declared impartiality, it still put up a resistance against people, which resulted in some murder and the ruining of public buildings.

Religious leaders were trying to convince people to hand over their arms; so far there was no success.

There have been some interviews with those authorities from the ex-regime who are now detained.

This is pleasing for those who suffered for years, but it revealed a terrible truth that the same would be repeated by the newcomers. They threatened the commander of the military government, but he did not change his mind and supported the Shah. He said, "I have sworn to be loyal."

Today there was a rumor that Palestinians captured the Shah in Morocco and will soon send him to Tehran to go on trial. But the news was denied. Foreign governments are recognizing the Bazargan government, one after another. Even the United States, which were friends of the Shah and were supporting him and Bakhtiar, recognize the new regime that is going to be an Islamic republic, and they reasoned that we are facing the reality in Iran. There was a flood of letters and telegrams addressed to the prime minister's office. They were competing in showing their faith before others do so.

Since this was the revolution of ordinary people that was rooted in dissatisfaction of the government and the defective leadership, there was no need to take long hours of radio and TV time and pages of newspapers full of congratulations to the new government. I wish they could give the revolution some time to do something and not repeat the same patterns of former governments.

Today seven ministers were introduced to Parliament. The situation is so complicated that there is no hope for betterment until the situation of runaway officers and soldiers and arms at the hands of irresponsible youth are solved. When the SAVAK prisons were taken by the people, some murderers and thieves were also released, and it is difficult to return them to prison.

Non-Iranians, especially Americans, are treated poorly. They are taken in groups and delivered to the imam's committee. People have killed some army generals and SAVAK employees. Pictures of them in terrible states are printed in the first pages of newspapers and shown on TV.

Shapour Bakhtiar and Khosrowdad, commander of the air force, are being detained by the people and were sent to the imam's committee. They have decided to arrest the ministers as well.

These are terrible days. There are dangers from enemies of the regime. Apparently Marxists and the National Front, and hundreds of other groups that cooperated with them so far, cannot agree on dividing the power. The decision was made to run a referendum to choose the type of government. Decisions were made beforehand, and it is certain that an Islamic republic will win the majority of votes.

FEBRUARY 14, 1979

Amid no leadership and chaos, orders that are broadcasted repeatedly cause worry for all. The new regime tries to gather the scattered army, gendarmerie, and police personnel and put them back to work. The ministries are being run by the deputy ministers. People who gained power have arrested the authorities and taken them to imam's committee. Those responsible authorities are not ready to work in this chaos and run the ministries.

Ayatollah Khomeini asked people not to make trouble for those who are not guilty. It has not been said who will make decisions about the accusations. They accuse all authorities of the ex-regime and take them to the imam's committee.

Today I tried to contact the Ministry of Industries and Mines. According to the instruction by the prime minister, I am responsible for the ministry until a minister is chosen. I was informed that the ministry was a warfront, was set on fire, and everything was looted. All windows are broken and the archives of the finance and industry offices are gone in the fire. Now some youth are guarding it and do not let anybody in.

The oppositions are killing the partners of the new regime. Ayatollah Khomeini ordered no more trouble for foreign embassies, but some people attacked the U.S. Embassy. Not having a disciplinary power caused the arrest of fifty Americans. Maybe the Americans will take action to save the lives of their people, which will cause more trouble.

FEBRUARY 16, 1979

Yesterday at the people's court, four army generals were investigated and sentenced to death. The sentence was carried out immediately. They were: Nematollah Nasiri, head of SAVAK; Khosrowdad, commander of the air force; Rahimi, army governor of Tehran; and Raji Isfahan, the army commander. The place of execution was the rooftop of the Alavi School, the residence of Ayatollah Khomeini. This hasty execution caused disappointment for those who expected to watch their trial and hear their explanations.

After four days of Bazargan's cabinet, disagreements started among them. Irregular troops are not ready to return the arms that they have taken from the barracks. They have organized a staff of partnership and are everywhere, such as at the courts and cabinet. They claim that they have caused victory of the revolution, and they are asking for their share in the results of the revolution.

The government announced that February 17

would be the end of the strikes and asked people go back to work. Maybe the order will not be followed, and there will be more demonstrations and possibly some killings.

TV programs were cut suddenly and by 9:45 PM stopped broadcasting; usually they continued until midnight. All responsible authorities of television were called to Tehran.

In Tabriz, they are still resisting; so far many have been killed. In the new regime, they do not talk about the number of people who are killed. .

There is no news about the promised freedom and democracy; everything is one sided. We do not know who is in the revolutionary court and people's council. Air force personnel and the police do not agree with the appointed commanders, and they are not ready to cooperate. It is possible that another crisis will happen in the air force.

The homes of rich people are being confiscated by the people from the Islamic Revolution and handed over to the Islamic government committees. One of the most luxurious homes belonged to one of the relatives of the Shah named Nahvi. The household was shown on TV and looked like a palace of a king in the nineteenth century. Immediately after that, they showed a film about the life of poor children in the desert in order to demonstrate the contrast between the two ways of life.

Those who left their homes and fled abroad or to other cities will lose their title and ownership. One hundred and twenty-eight ministers and authorities of the ex-regime were arrested. Their properties will be confiscated and they will possibly be executed. It is possible that Shapour Bakhtiar is among them. He has been popular because of the courage he showed in the most critical days of his country. They call him a real philanthropist. If he is executed, they will face a protest by the people.

The critical positions of the country, such as in radio, TV, and telecommunication, are at the disposal of people with left wing tendencies. They have cooperated with Khomeini on a common goal, which was toppling the Shah. It is not clear what they will do later. Universities that are the hiding place of intellectuals are very hard to take over. Ghotbzadeh, a friend of Ayatollah Khomeini, was appointed to the director of TV. About this, he said, "Stop being intellectual; everything will be purely Islamic, and radio is only for giving messages of revolution."

The position of the press is not yet clear; it is doubtful that they can have the freedom they enjoyed before the revolution.

Now we are living in a city that has no proper government, law, army, or even police. People are worried about the great number of arms that are at the hands of the people. The efforts of the revolutionary government did not work on returning them. Such a crisis never happened in any revolution. It is not an easy job to gather the scattered army.

Oil production for export has not yet started. A test flight by Iran Air has been started. The United States and the United Kingdom started the evacuation of their citizens from Iran.

FEBRUARY 18, 1979

Yesterday was the start of my work. I went to the Ministry of Industries and Mines to introduce myself to the new minister and resign from my job. I was so sad to see the front, where 160 people were killed. I was so upset that I wanted to cry.

Another deputy minister came with me to the gathering of the employees. They called us remains of the ex-regime and faced us with absolute cruelty and impolite statements. They sent us to a revolution committee. In the committee, they asked us to show them documents. As they did not have anything bad on us, they released us. They locked our rooms so that we could not have access to our files.

I am happy that I worked so honestly and that the worst of enemies could not present a document against me. The truth is that this is a period of transfer of power, and I should understand it. I am sure that days of excitement will pass and reasoning will replace it, and the honest and dishonest individuals will be recognized.

When I came back home, I had many telephone calls from employees of the ministry who expressed their pity about the behavior of some of the colleagues. The same scenario happened in other ministries, universities, and government offices. This was a revolutionary instruction. It was better for me not to be involved in such an environment. In my heart, I wish that what was good for the people would come through. I imagine that to pretend to be a revolutionary is a wrong idea. Moreover, it is too soon to judge the situation. Anyway, my new lifestyle has begun. I have to learn how to use my time in the best way.

Today the first foreign guest of Bazargan's government, Yasser Arafat, leader of the Palestine Free Movement, arrived in Tehran and visited Ayatollah Khomeini. The visit has cleared the foreign policy of the new government and revealed that they will be real leftists that are going to make a terrible unity in the Middle East and threaten United States, Israel, and their Arab friends. Even though the United States has evacuated seven thousand of its citizens from Iran, it still wants to cooperate with the Bazargan government. However, it seems that there is no room for the United States and United Kingdom; maybe the new regime will be a friend of Russia.

Almost every army general is detained and all ranks above colonel are retired. Recently two generals were appointed but immediately replaced with two colonels.

It is possible that more of the authorities from the Shah's regime are getting executed. All properties of the Shah and his authorities were confiscated, and every transaction on these properties has been forbidden.

The Islamic government has asked Morocco to return the Shah to Iran to undergo trial. It is not clear what the reaction of Morocco will be. They have created such a hate for the Shah in every country that they also do not accept him.

FEBRUARY 20, 1979

It is arranged that the schools open today. We do not know what is going to happen. Yesterday, Ayatollah Khomeini expressed his deep regret about the event that is going on in Kurdistan. The government speaker strongly denies the separation of Kurdistan.

Censorship and suffocation has a new appearance. They do not tell people what they do not like. This fact was announced by the director of the TV organization. At present, the organization is at the disposal of Ayatollah Khomeini's staff, and they only broadcast news about him. Ayatollah Khomeini's speech was unilateral and revolutionary. It is expected that the staff of the TV organization that worked so hard for having freedom do not agree with it. They cut his speech with the "Allah Akbar" slogan.

Today a few of the army generals went on trial in the revolutionary court and were later executed. People do not know who members of the Revolutionary Court are and they are not informed of their decisions. Fadaeian Khalgh, a party who had a great share in the movement, has announced that they will have demonstrations for two days and protest the kind of investigations going on. In some newspapers, there are protests. Referendum becomes a funny subject.

In schools, there are only speeches and debates. There is protest against the contents of textbooks. Children are getting involved in politics and they do not like to sit down and study.

FEBRUARY 21, 1978

People are protesting about not having freedom of speech and gathering. Yesterday and today it was repeatedly announced that some people are carrying Ayatollah's picture and marching toward his home. Ayatollah announced that these people are not Muslim, and people should not cooperate with them. The same people that are called non-Muslims are those who had a great share in the change of the regime. Now they are elected from radio and TV, and Ayatollah banned their demonstrations. Soon the newspapers will face suffocation and all efforts for reaching democracy will result in dictatorship.

Dr. Reza Baraheni, who is of the opposition and for years fought in the United States against the Shah, wrote a very hard article about Ghotbzadeh, the director of TV, and the others followed him.

Foreign governments are protesting the procedure of the revolutionary courts. The situation in prison for those who cooperated with the Shah's regime is terrible. As prisons are ruined, they are in very bad situations. In the courts, they hit prisoners and assault them; they do not respond to their questions and do not let them defend themselves. Ayatollah Taleghani criticized the way they are treating the prisoners and said that he is not participating in these courts; he made a very interesting statement about freedom for every human being.

FEBRUARY 23, 1979

It was expected that the secret courts and execution orders in private have stopped, but last night, once again an army commander was executed. Bazargan, the prime minister, said that the execution has taken place by the order of his superior. By saying this, he expressed that he has no power and authority in his job.

In the press, there was news about the conspiracy of an army general named Tavakoli with an American general Sharon. Sharon resigned after disclosure of the conspiracy and said that tapes of Tavakoli's voice and his notes are available.

Some terrible news has been spread about the breakdown of the country. Kurdistan announced its self-control, and it is said that parts of Iran, Turkey, and Iraq will be in their territory, and Palestinians will be settled there. Apparently, the Palestinians are gong to replace the foreign technicians in the oil industries. If that happens, it will be a great danger for the independence of Iranian oil.

It has been about one week since I have been at

home, and I am happy with reading books. All my friends and relatives are reading books because there is nothing to do.

For the first time, there was no ceremony about the coup d'état of Reza Shah, and the related formalities did not happen. It was funny that there was an article in a newspaper proving that Reza Shah was an illegitimate child and felt sorry for those who were ruled by an illegitimate Shah.

Natural spring approaches along with the political spring. I wish the political spring does not result in dictatorship. Only very optimistic people can look forward to a better environment. The future is so ambiguous that I do not dare to be hopeful.

FEBRUARY 26, 1979

In response to the question of a retired judge, Ayatollah Khomeini stated that the Family Protection Law is contrary with the Koran and should not be followed. In a country where the left wing speaks about human rights, the Family Protection Law is annulled by one sentence from Ayatollah Khomeini. The law gave women the conditional right by court to divorce, have custody of children, and legalized polygamy. Although the courts were chaired by men with prejudice, it was still a venue for women who were abused by husbands. The government claims that it supports the underprivileged people; still, the law that was protective of the same women has been annulled by the leader. Educated women and well-off women have little problem with alimony and divorce.

Ayatollah Khomeini stated that every Muslim country should go under one government and one flag. This means there would be no tribal and minority groups. They will eradicate the Iranian flag and all the traditional Iranian ceremonies. So far, no two Muslim countries have been united, even for a short time.

Bazargan had a weak stand in front of the imam's committees that have absolute power.

They run courts, execute people, and confiscate their belongings. The government is busy with minor problems and does not know what is going on.

FEBRUARY 28, 1978

Gradually people have started to express their feelings and ask for freedom. *Ayandegan* (a newspaper) insists on its stand and will continue on its own way. They started to print interesting articles by people. They all wanted freedom and protests against arrests and executions by the imam's committees in Tehran and in the provinces.

It is decided that on March 5, 1978, which is the anniversary of Dr. Mohammad Mosaddegh's passing away, the first shipment of oil is to be sent abroad. So far we do not know about the policies of export and production of oil. It is certain that no new privileges are given to consortium companies, and production will not reach its maximum. In the world markets, oil is sold at a price higher than what OPEC has decided, so some countries will have to reduce their consumption.

Dr. Nazih, chairman of the Lawyers Association, was appointed as managing director of the National Oil Company. He is an intelligent and experienced man. If things go on like this, there is hope that he could be successful. This year it is announced that the anniversary of Dr. Mosaddegh will be held with special ceremonies at his tomb at Ahmad Abad. That means that they are going to celebrate the nationalization of oil after twenty-five years.

Today Ayatollah Khomeini announced that he has hired commandos to return the Shah to Iran. He also chose a stadium with the capacity of a hundred thousand for his trial site.

Commandos are assigned to return all the escaped Iranians back to Iran. Egypt's president, Anvarsadat, stated that the Shah may stay in Egypt like an ordinary man. Some prisoners of Heshmatieh who were detained for corruption escaped the prison in the days of the revolution when the prison was on fire have not yet been arrested.

People push for freedom of the media. It seems that there is breeze of freedom because some of the groups were allowed to express their views. At present, TV shows are mostly revolutionary songs, the committee's announcement, and some war films. Radio has a better position. If there is freedom, people may express interesting views that will enrich the programs.

Ghotbzadeh, who came to Iran accompanying Ayatollah Khomeini, was assigned to the position of director general of Radio and Television. A wave of protest started at this. Nobody was able to create such a chaos in such a short time and disgrace themselves like that. People speak about his background and say that he speaks like a dictator. The staff of Radio and Television, who played a great role in the revolution, is not ready for such behavior. He should change his manners or there will be another crisis.

Yesterday, Moinfar, a minister without portfolio, was appointed for supervision of the Ministry of Industries and Mines. I do not know how one person can handle two very responsible jobs.

MARCH 2, 1978

Ayatollah Khomeini announced that he wants to go to Ghom (the holy city) where people will welcome him. Faizieh School (a school for clergies) that was closed during the Shah's reign will be reopened. Ayatollah Khomeini sent a message that was like a testimonial; he recommended many ethical and religious points. At the same time, he said, "What I want is an Islamic republic, no more, no less," which shows he has not yielded to the wish of the left wing that wanted a democratic republic.

Ayatollah Khomeini said, the "justice system does not work properly. Ministries should come out of the palaces. All the teachers who were working during exploitation regime should be dismissed. The type of government should be Islamic republic. We build houses for poor, avoid selling at high prices," and he gave more instructions.

It is decided that more leadership authority was given to Ayatollah Taleghani. He is a very logical, intellectual, and decisive man and is acceptable to all groups. He chose to go into prison instead of going on exile. For sixteen years, he was in SAVAK prison and did not change his mind. During his detention, he socialized with many and became clear-sighted.

In a T.V. interview, Engineer Bazargan, the premier, spoke about the troubles that the committees assigned by Ayatollah Khomeini are making for him, and he said he cannot work with such a system. Committees try people in provinces and sentence them to death; they do this very fast in a way that there are only a few days between the trial and execution of the order. Committees do not stop this kind of punishment, although there are many protests against it.

After twenty-five years in exile, Dr. Shayegan came to Iran as a candidate for presidency. In his first interview, he said, "We cannot have Islamic government. The type of government should be voted for by the people." This statement was not welcomed by the authorities.

MARCH 5, 1978

Today was a great day for Iranian people. Twelve years after the passing away of Dr. Mosaddegh, they gathered around his resting place and appreciated his services. Ten thousand people went to Ahmad Abad and apologized for the ingratitude extended to him. Some forgot Dr. Mosaddegh, who made sacrifices to make Iran free and tried to nationalize oil. Among this generation are the people who caused trouble for Iran by letting him down.

I do no not know why we are always late and lack courage. But we are ready for ruining each other and weep for the dead. The situation is similar to Dr. Mosaddegh's time. Some are surrounding Ayatollah Khomeini and doing wrong things in his name, until he is totally corrupted.

The government is not fully in power and works in isolation. There are many prisoners that there is no information about.

Today I visited the new minister of the Ministry of Industries and Mines. His name is Ahmadzadeh; he is an impatient and temperamental man. He is under the influence of some employees who call themselves representatives of others. He found my weak point in accepting a job with the ex-regime. He agreed to return me to the Central Bank of Iran. It was obvious that he was not ready for reasoning. I made no effort to defend myself. It is a blessing to be far away from the chaos atmosphere.

Today the first of export oil was sold to Japan in the name of Dr. Mosaddegh. It was decided that the proceeds go for the welfare of oil employees and development of Khuzestan.

MARCH 9, 1978

Yesterday was International Women's Day. In Ghom, Ayatollah Khomeini announced that women should wear full hijab in the offices. While women around the world are working for freedom and the equality of rights, Iranian women are returned to forty years ago and ordered to go back to their own homes. The reaction of women was interesting. Even women with maghnae (half hijab) were angry about being forced to wear hijab. Certain activities, judiciary jobs, and service in the army were forbidden for women.

A group of women marched toward the prime minister's office and the home of Ayatollah Taleghani and demonstrated in the streets. Tear gas was used on them, and they were hit with stones. Women without hijab were insulted in the streets. The prime minister did not talk to women and reasoned that this was a unilateral decision by Ayatollah Khomeini. Ayatollah insulted teachers and the staff of radio and television. He said educational centers are houses of prostitutes. Those who empowered the regime are under his attack. There is a difference of opinion among members of National Front. Mojahedin and Fadaeean Khalgh, two political groups, have separated themselves from the regime and are unhappy about not sharing decision making. The resignation of Bazargan was denied. A prime minister who does not know what is going on and faces new problems every day has every right to declare his irresponsibility.

If women are united, they could be a huge power. The obligation of social service for women was annulled, and they have been dismissed from service. They say a woman can be president, but then they cancel the Family Protection Law and force the veil on them.

At present there is no sign of the freedom that was promised. People do not have the right to smoke and choose their own clothes. Alcoholic beverages are collected and even non-Muslims and foreigners can not find them. They burn meats that are not slaughtered the Islamic way. Right now there is no chicken or meat available to the people.

The minister in charge of Revolution Affairs stated that, "We have food storage for thirty-three days." I do not understand how he calculated the amount of food storage and consumption of food that he was able to come up with that number.

All businessmen in export and import are already bankrupt or have taken their money out of the country. Those who remain do not dare to spend money in the chaos of business because every day they face a new rule.

Government offices cannot do a thing because of the strikes and because all the responsible authorities have been dismissed. Ministers are busy with the dismissal of those who worked with the ex-regime.

The New Year (Norooz) bonus is only 2,500 tomans for employees, which is not enough to purchase special items for Norooz. They do not care about national days and have reduced amount of the days off. There is no respect for Norooz. Heavy snow also helped the case of neglecting Norooz.

MARCH 11, 1979

The Iranian Revolution was for the achievement of freedom, but every day a new order is issued to limit individual and social freedom. The last order was the wearing of hijab for women, which faced a serious reaction, and they modified it.

The following cases are signs of freedom limitation:

- existence of the imam's committees that work beyond the government system and Justice Administration,
- wearing of the hijab for women in the workplace and on the streets,
- annulment of the Family Protection Law,
- forbidding consumption of meats that are not slaughtered in an Islamic way,
- forbidding alcoholic beverages for Muslims and non-Muslims,
- collecting cigarettes that are made in foreign countries,
- not allowing gatherings, except for believers of Ayatollah Khomeini,
- compelling people to vote for the Islamic republic,
- stopping women from travelling abroad without having permission from their husbands,
- forbidding mixed schools,
- forbidding the use of media by different groups,

- forbidding newspapers that print critical articles and censorship of books, newspapers, and films.

MARCH 13, 1979

The recommendation of the hijab for women in the offices has had a very serious reaction. A great number of women gathered in front of the Justice Administration and claimed that having the hijab is a violation of freedom. They asked for equal right in social, economical, and civic fields.

Some of the religious leaders, including Ayatollah Taleghani, explained that the purpose of the hijab for women was for their dignity. In front of the prime minister's office, women were scattered by tear gas. In response to their written complaint, they stated that they are free to wear whatever they want. A great number of women gathered in front of the television and protested against the not showing of the film of their demonstration. The director of Television made some stupid statement and at last showed the film, and then he invited the clergy to respond to the women's claims. Some funny reasons were brought up for not showing the demonstration of the women, such as there was sister of Shrif Imamy (the chairman of the senate now in prison) and a film artist among the women, and that they did not want to cause a misunderstanding with viewers. They then set punishments for those who made the trouble.

It was an untimely announcement that surprised everyone. Why in a country with too many problems would they raise the subject of the hijab that hurts many women and men? It gives an excuse to those who said they have given blood to achieve freedom. Maybe they have to change their promise about a referendum and give more freedom to people to choose their type of government.

Islamic demonstrations caused some doubt. Mojahedin, Marxists, and the Toudeh (People) Party, who did not gain their fair share from the revolution, will not give up easily. With the way that Ayatollah Khomeini and his followers are preaching, there is no doubt they will reach the majority of votes for the Islamic republic.

These days there are rumors that Ayatollah Khomeini was supported by Americans. If it is true, there will be more hardship for the left wings.

MARCH 14, 1979

Jaffarian and Nikkhah were executed for being close to the Shah, committing treacherous acts with the Toudeh Party, and writing articles against Ayatollah Khomeini. The hasty executions are being protested by the people. The prisons are full of detainees who were protesting executions. The Red Cross has interfered.

The problem of the hijab has been almost forgotten by women. They said that the hijab is not a compulsory issue. Now there are protests against the visit of President Carter in Cairo. Yasser Arafat and his ambassador in Tehran have a big share in what is going on in Iran. Dr. Sanjabi, the minister of foreign affairs, has resigned.

It is expected that Ayatollah Khomeini will grant a general pardon and relieve the detainees. So far, the justice system is not in the picture. The reason for the necessity of a general grant may be that the number of people who did not work in the ex-regime is so few, and they are not able to work with such a small group. They must find a way to run the country and excuse some people who worked for the ex-regime.

Last night was the last Wednesday of the year and a traditional ceremony for end of the year, but there was no sign of day. This Norooz will not be the same because it is the fortieth day of the movement in which thousands were killed.

MARCH 21, 1979

A year full of adventure passed, and the first day of spring arrived. I hope we can say good-bye to the old year and hope for better days. The first program of the year was the remembrance of victims and sympathy for their families. People have mixed feelings; they do not know whether to be happy or sorry. They are happy for Norooz and sorry for what they have lost. There are families that lost their members in the revolution, others who are far from home in exile.

The problem with Kurdistan is in a new phase. People occupied government offices in Sanandaj, and the government bombarded them. They think the problem is solved; it is not that easy. The Kurds are fighting for autonomy. The same is true with other minorities. Workers ask for a raise, and the homeless ask the government to make shelters for them. So far nothing is being done; they only try to cover their mistakes.

For Norooz, I was with my family in Sari. When I go back to Tehran, I will start my new plan. My retirement has not yet finalized, but it is clear that I should yield my position. I will establish a translation office to help those who are leaving the country, and at the same time, I shall work on a book translation. At the moment, the situation is just waiting and seeing. One day they will look for experienced people to help them.

The city has referendum fever. They change their ideas every day. First, the question was the constitution or an Islamic republic. Then it changed to an Islamic republic: yes or no? Propaganda for an Islamic republic is so wide and strong that they will win the case. So far nobody knows what an Islamic republic is. Women are afraid of having more limitations. Some groups have banned voting. The legal age is reduced to sixteen years. It has been decided that the referendum is done as of March 10. We can foresee the result ahead of time: Ayatollah Khomeini stated that he will vote for it and encouraged the others to follow him.

The government has given privileges to Kurdistan in order to stop the chaos. The same may happen in other provinces, such as Khuzestan, Baluchistan, and Azerbaijan.

London Radio read a message from Shapour Bakhtiar, the ex-prime minister, in which he criticized the referendum, Bazargan, and Ayatollah Khomeini. Since the new government has been elected, the view on Bakhtiar has changed. Intellectuals call him a liberal and philanthropist, while Ayatollah Khomeini called him "corrupted on Earth." I think Bakhtiar has escaped from the country.

MARCH 30, 1979

The referendum is done. The voting sheet said: "Islamic Republic, Yes or No." Propaganda was so wide that people had a very nice picture of an Islamic republic. Radio and Television unilaterally encouraged people to vote for an Islamic republic. Hundreds were interviewed; none of them had a proper idea. They voted because they were Muslim. Some university students and teachers and some parties banned the referendum. The result was known ahead of time anyway. A constitution is an important factor but nobody knows about it. Before asking about a constitution, they made a referendum for the type of government. They asked people to vote in the dark.

In some provinces, such as Kurdistan, Baluchestan, and Khuzestan, there are riots. The worst was in the city of Gonbadkavous. The government used the army to stop the riot.

Today Dr. Madani, the minister of defense, resigned. Two days ago, General Gharanay, head of the army staff, was dismissed because of rumors about him. So far the army is not in good shape and has no commander.

The big problem is the promises that were given to poor people and not fulfilled. If the promises are not realized in a short time, it will annoy them and possibly cause protest against the government. Every day the followers of Ayatollah Khomeini diminish. Contradictions from the people close to him have caused problems. It seems that Ghotbzadeh and Banisadr, close friends of Ayatollah, are trying to create disappointment among the people.

APRIL 2, 1979

Ayatollah Khomeini announced April 1 as the day of the martyred and the beginning of an Islamic republic. We know nothing about the constitution. They are going to announce it later. In fact, people agreed to an Islamic republic not knowing about their constitution. After the referendum, BBC Radio announced, "that was a vote of confidence to Ayatollah Khomeini."

Around the country there are riots; the most serious

one is in Gonbadkavous. There is a real war between the government and the Turkmens. It lasted nine days. After the government ultimatum that they stop the war, the assistant army will go to Gonbadkaous. Apparently a ceasefire has been accepted by the two parties, the prisoners were released, and the wounded cured.

The big problem of Gondabkaous is the common border with Russia, and it is said that the arms come from Russia. Fadaeian Khalgh (a Marxist group) entered the war in favor of Turkmens. Fadaein Khalgh had a big role in toppling the Shah, but now they are going to be separated from Islamists and are ready to go undercover. Now that they have been recognized in the demonstrations, they will easily be trapped.

Today they asked people to forget about the thirteenth of Farvardin (a national day for going on picnics and celebrating the renewal of nature) and to go to the cemeteries to put flowers on the tombs of martyrs. People went for picnics, and those who had a martyr in the family left red tulips on their resting places at the cemeteries.

As of today, the Iranian government is officially a republic. They claim they will work for poor people and respect the rights of minorities, such as Kurds, Lors, Turkmens, and Balouchs. They will give women equal rights as men, and there will be more promises that we have to wait and see.

APRIL 9, 1979

Every day the revolutionary courts execute people. Two days ago they murdered Hoveyda, the ex-prime minister. He stated that he had not read the bill of indictment and had no opportunity to defend himself. A spirit of revenge has awakened in people. Through propaganda, people feel happy about executions. For thirteen years, Hoveyda was the prime minister, and dissatisfaction was high. There were many possibilities at the disposal of the government, and he did very little for the people. Courts should act according to the bylaw approved by the revolution council, but they do not consider it. The bylaw was not satisfactory to the minister of justice.

The high prices are unbelievable. Today Ayatollah Khomeini issued an order to fight against high prices. The opportunists can adjust themselves with any environment. The problem of losing jobs is resurfacing as well. Apparently, no quick solution is on the way. Most of the industries are stopped, and there are no investments by public or private sectors.

The problem of minorities and their demand for autonomy is not solved. The government promised them that it would be considered in the constitution. In Azerbaijan, they have already started a plan, and they are publishing a newspaper in the Azari language.

APRIL 9, 1979

The revolutionary courts work day and night, and they are often killing people. The government approves the punishment of these people and knows nothing about the procedure in the courts.

Those who are sentenced to death are mostly from the army, police, and gendarmerie who were involved with killings. Recently they spread a list of forty people who were arrested. Some SAVAK documents fell in the hands of people, and they made arrests of people involved.

The problem of unemployment is not solved. Every day groups of people gather in front of the Justice

Administration or Ministry of Labor. There is no shortcut solution for the problem. Ayatollah Khomeini issued an order that he will treat those who sell their commodities at high price according Islamic laws. The income reduction of individuals, diminishing supply and rising of prices are causing frustration.

Ayatollah Taleghani, the respected personality, has closed his office and went to an unknown place. Committees have made problems for his son and daughter-in-law. The role of Ayatollah Taleghani in solving people's problems and his mediation in contradictions was very important. It is not clear what would be the reaction of his many followers to the response of the government. His existence was really valuable for defusing the fires.

Turkmens asked for his intermediation. So far, the trip is not done. The problem of the Turkmens and the injustices to them are not easy to resolve, and they need delicate diplomacy.

APRIL 15, 1979

There is chaos about what the Revolutionary Committee did to Ayatollah Taleghani's family. Newspapers and the government are involved in this problem. In the city, there were some demonstrations in favor of Ayatollah Taleghani. The revolution will face many problems if Taleghani is out of it, such as the separation of the followers of him and the followers of Ayatollah Khomeini. A revolution public prosecutor cancelled all membership cards of the committees and prohibited the arrest of people and the searching of their homes.

APRIL 20, 1979

Ayatollah Khomeini announced April 19 as the Day of the Army. He suggested that the army march through the streets. There was no discipline among them. People were riding on tanks and trucks in civilian dress. Most soldiers had heavy beards and some had no hats. People were offering them flowers, and they put the flowers on their guns with very sad faces. There was no type of army discipline in the march. I hope the enemies are not using this low spirit against Iran.

Killing by the revolution committees continue in the provinces. After the disposal of the chiefs, it is time for getting rid of the police and lower-ranking army personnel. Nobody had seen faces of the members of the revolutionary committees, and nobody dares to tell them to stop killing.

A protest by Ayatollah Taleghani caused new trouble, and people came to the streets with loud slogans and ready for a riot. Ayatollah Taleghani asked people not to make gatherings. Today he visited Ayatollah Khomeini, and he promised to tell the truth to the people. Revolutionary Council committees and the government claim to be innocent and say that some secret hands are working to make a separation among the followers of Ayatollah Khomeini.

Unemployment among intellectuals and well-educated people is as bad as unemployment among workers who used their life savings. The educated people care for their prestige; the psychological aspect of unemployment is worse than the financial impact. This group of people lost their jobs for no reason, and they can cause great problems for society. Due to the pride and prejudice of those in power, they have no time for these people.

The government has no solution for restarting factories and offices, unless they give immunity to those that were expelled.

All industrialist and high-ranking employees in the government were not corrupt. They were working with the regime, and their big sin was not protesting the ruling government.

Those poor people that are under government protection can do nothing by themselves to start the economy of the country.

It is said that the money from the sold oil has not yet been collected; signs of a shortage of funds are clear everywhere. The method of this government is being criticized by foreign spectators. No hand is stretched toward this fanatical regime. Within the government, some conflicts exist. The constitution is not yet published, and it has been delayed for some time. Left wings are getting close together, and all select Ayatollah Taleghani for leadership. He is the one that is most offended by the regime.

APRIL 25, 1979

In Tehran, the Revolutionary Court has stopped killing, but in provinces they kill people every day. The government tries to collect the arms and centralize the works of the police and army.

Those who enjoyed having arms do not agree with this decision.

Two days ago, General Ghareney, who was the head of the army staff and fully authorized by Ayatollah Khomeini, was assassinated by a group of terrorists. They claimed that his crime was attachment to imperialism and involvement in the murders in Kurdistan.

His body was buried with full ceremony in Ghom. The prime minster stated that he was an honor to the Islamic republic and expressed deep sadness. This was the fourth political assassination.

Prime Minister Bazargan asked people to stop revenge and pardon those who cooperated with the ex-regime. He presented some phrases from the Koran on being kind. He said, "I have nothing to do with the Revolutionary Council," which means they do not listen to him.

So far the method of work at the Revolutionary Court has not changed. Sometimes they show the accused people on TV. Judges, however, are unknown and have covered faces.

Yesterday, people had a demonstration supporting Ayatollah Shariatmadari, who denied the Islamic republic and supported a republic of Khalghe Mosalman (a leftist group). He has decided to immigrate to Egypt.

Ayatollah Taleghani visited with Ayatollah Khomeini regarding what happened to his children, and then he returned to his camp. He went to Naghedeh to negotiate with people who entered an internal war that resulted in heavy loss between the Turks and Kurds. The conflicts ended when they were threatened about army interference.

Pressure and suffocation of the media is continuing. Two newspapers, *Payghame Emrouz* and *Ahangar,* which wrote critical texts, were attacked and forced to close. *Khandaniha* magazine has been stopped; nobody knows where the owner Amirani has gone and what his crime is.

TV shows are below standard, and the staff are

protesting and creating no new programs. Director Ghotbzadeh has given five days time to those who worked for SAVAK to show up and introduce themselves. The threats have no effects and cannot solve the problem of those who have no understanding with the director.

After the resignation of Dr. Sanjabi, Dr. Yazdi was assigned to the position of foreign minister. There are plenty of rumors about Dr. Yazdi, such as him having an American passport. He explained that his Iranian passport was expired, and he was forced to get an American passport but he remained Iranian. It is possible that Revolutionary Committee gets weaker in the absence of Dr. Yazdi.

The police have started functioning, but the members lack self-confidence. They fear they will be murdered because of accusations of working with the ex-regime.

MAY 2, 1979

Around 6:00 PM, when I was working at the Takht-e Tavoos Translation Office, my husband arrived and said that two people were asking for me. I asked, "Are they from the Committee?" He answered, "Yes." A man with an order for my arrest from the Revolutionary Prosecutor's Office and two armed individuals took me to the committee at Zafar Avenue. Before this, they inspected my home and took some papers and photographs with them. First, they said a representative from the prosecutor's office would talk to me. After two hours, they took me to another place; I do not know where it was, because I was blindfolded. When they asked my specifications, they detained me with folded eyes. The room was big and clean. I could not sleep that night even with a sleeping pill. They never told me what my crime was and how long I would be detained. When I was in the car, the driver asked me about my relationship with Zahedi (the Iranian ambassador to the United States), and how long I have lived in the United States. He also asked about Mahnaz Afkhami (the minister in charge of Women's Affairs) and Najmabadi (the minister of Industries and Mines). I had no information on them. He asked whether I was working during Azahari's time; my answer was yes.

On the wall of the cell, there is a printed paper in Arabic that reads: "Revenge brings life to you." I do not know why I should be subject to revenge. I have served the society with honesty and sincerity. I am sure that it is hard for my husband and my children to see what has happened to me; God will help them.

Last night they gave me dinner and in the morning a breakfast. Whenever I need a washroom, they take me in a blindfold. Doors and windows are tightly closed, just like a prison.

I should wait and be patient. I have nothing in my handbag to keep me busy. I watch the door to see when the interrogator will arrive to at least tell me what my crime was.

I read poetry I have known by heart. I try to look to my life and find where I was wrong, what I could have done and what I should not have done. I do not regret my life; my services will compensate my mistakes. I am afraid my husband will have a heart attack. I think of my children who appreciated my works.

It is hard to spend time in detention. To calm myself, I try to think about those who are suffering life sentences and torture. How cruel are people to each other? They want us to think the same way that they do. The Islamic republic requires this, and so did the ex-regime. You should either stay and compromise or fight and go to prison.

At last, I got a book from Banisadr (the president) about Iran's economy. For a few hours, I had something to do.

MAY 19, 1979

While I was in detention, the Pasdaran inspected my home and my bedroom. They took away a photo album, telephone book, a report that I had written for submission to the Status of Women Commission in the United Nations, and a few newspapers with my picture on them.

I do not know where I was detained. People with covered faces asked odd questions. They have taken me to be a very important person in contact with those they are looking for. They asked how long I was in the United States and why I became secretary general of the Women's Organization and deputy minister. They asked about my salary and my relationship with SAVAK. All my answers were right. They observed that after 34 years of service I was living in an apartment with six other people. I am sure they have done a complete investigation on my assets and the way I was serving the people.

They were looking for people who had complaints against me, and that was all in vain. At last, they let me go with the guarantee that my husband and I would go back when they called. They told me that I wouldn't know my fate until Sunday.

Twenty days have now passed, and I have heard nothing from them, but their heavy shadow is spread over my life and my attitude. I hate my bedroom. I feel sick when I think some pasdars (guards) have gone through my personal items. I cannot say that I regret my services, but I can say that I am really upset to see that there is no difference between those who worked honestly and those who were corrupted. By their inhumane conduct, they cause all specialists to leave the country. There is a sign of cooperation with ex-regime on the forehead of many of the best intellectuals of this country.

I am happy that they did not keep me more than twenty-four hours. But, I do not feel immune. Every day I expect to be called for more investigations and for them to move me from one place to another with a blindfold. After what happened to me, I am doubtful about continuing these notes. I am afraid that one day they will be used against me. I also do not like to leave these notes incomplete. The rest is written for my son, who is studying in the United States and wishes to come back to his own country and serve his own people. I do not see that happening in the present situation.

While I stopped writing, the most important event was the assassination of Ayatollah Motahari, chief of the Revolution Court and the closest friend and colleague of Ayatollah Khomeini. His murder made people mourn for a week. Apparently this was done by the same group who assassinated Gharenay.

The head of the Revolution Committee has ordered the killing of the Shah and his relatives. They announced that they would award a trip to Mecca to the Shah's killer. That is why the countries are hesitant to accept the Shah as a refugee.

Every day something happens in Khuzestan. Committees, centers, and associations are dissolved. *Ayandegan* was closed by the order of Ayatollah Khomeini. *Keyhan* has expelled its editorial council. Workers are taking over the newspaper. In the days that they are about to put the constitution on referendum, limitation of newspapers is hard for the intellectuals and worries them.

The prime minister asked the government employees to give them minimum salary and to try to behave revolutionary, since they have not collected the oil money. Radio and TV have nothing to say except religious matters. Nobody has more enemies than the director of TV. Some humorous newspapers made some caricatures of him. There are plenty of rumors about Ghotbzadeh and Ebrahim Yazdi.

MAY 23, 1979

The United States Senate has passed a bill by consensus and condemned the slaughters by the Islamic Revolutionary Courts. The relationship between Iran and the United States is in the worst possible state. Iran has asked the United States not to send their ambassador to Iran until the situation is cleared. In Iran wide demonstrations happened, and it will continue for two days. The foreign secretary of the United States said, "This is not the feeling of Iranian people," and hopes that the misunderstanding is somehow removed.

Ayatollah Khomeini said the relationship between Iran and the United States is the relationship of an oppressor and the oppressed. We do not need to have such relationship with United States.

There seems to be some changes in the procedures of the Revolutionary Courts, such as forgiving the seventy arrested Parliament representatives. It was asked that they return the money they made during their term and confess to their crimes. Some of them accepted the conditions, and the others mentioned the salary was paid for their services.

The resignation of Ayatollah Khalkhali, chair of the Revolutionary Committee who ordered the assassination of the Shah and his family, caused some trouble. He said nobody is allowed to ask him questions.

Today they announced that Revolutionary guards are not entitled to arrest army and police personnel. This should be done by the army.

The political environment is terrible. There is no news about the six-hour meeting of the Revolutionary Committee and the cabinet in the presence of Ayatollah Khomeini.

So far the most problematic issue of the day is the TV organization. Almost all the personnel are on strike. There are some doubts about the expenses incurred by the organization.

There was great protest inside and outside of Iran about the closing of *Ayadegen*. At last, the newspaper started again. *Keyhan* is in the hands of workers right now, and the editorial staff is on strike. Recent issues of the newspaper were in vain and published under a shadow of fear.

MAY 26, 1979

Every day the situation gets worse. Yesterday a great demonstration against the United States happened in Tehran and the provinces. They burned the U.S. flag in front of the embassy and some puppets of Carter, Begin, Israel's prime minister, and Uncle Sam. They shouted awful slogans against the American Senate and Carter.

Ayatollah Khomeini stated that, "We do not need the United States; we have internal enemies such as the National Front and the left wing. Whoever wants something besides the party of the Islamic republic is an enemy of Islam." In his speech, he protested against

Dr. Mosaddegh. In a meeting of one hundred thousand people in the Industrial University, warm feelings were shown toward Mosaddegh, and the reaction for Ayatollah Khomeini was not the same as it was before.

Ayatollah Rafsanjani, a friend and supporter of Ayatollah Khomeini, was targeted for assassination, but he escaped safely. So far the reality is not disclosed, but the attempts were recognized. This made Ayatollah Khomeini more furious; his reaction is expected.

Ayatollah Khomeini asked the prime minister to expedite approval of the constitution. So far, the text that has been distributed has raised many complaints. The constitution has been put in referendum instead of going to the Experts Council. It is expected that the same method of "Islamic Republic: Yes or No" will be used, and there will be no chance for any complaint. Ayatollah Khomeini intends this law to be purely Islamic and in compliance with the Koran. I do not know where in the Koran the type of government and constitution is mentioned. In my view, the Human Rights Charter should be observed by all governments.

So far there is no reaction from the American side with regard to the assaults made on them. It seems that they do not like to get involved.

Shortage of fuel in the United States is becoming a big problem. People wait for hours in line for gas. If the political aspect overcomes the economic aspect and the sale of oil is cut to Americans, then we will have no wheat and they will have no oil.

JUNE 2, 1979

War is getting hot in Khuzestan. The Arabs want self-autonomy. The Pasdaran (the guardians) were sent to Khuzestan to help the army. Over four days, a riot in

Khoramshahr killed twenty and others were wounded. General Madani, the governor and commander of the marine forces, tried to distinguish the fire. It is said that Libyans and Iraqis went to Khuzestan to support the Arabs.

Lawyers protested the method of voting for the constitution. Ayatollah Khomeini ordered a copy of the law forwarded to the Lawyers Association for their comments. There are some conflicts among lawyers and clergies.

Khalkhali, who no longer is the chief of the Revolutionary Committee, has gone to Dubai and made statements about changing the name of the Persian Gulf to the Islamic Gulf and giving three islands (two Tombs and Abumousa) to the United Arab Emirates, which caused protest by the foreign minister and serious objection by Iranians.

The protest against the United States has almost diminished, and the Americans ignored it. Clergies are working in the Revolutionary Committees. Today they executed three people. They said there are many who should go under investigation in this court.

Some people want candidate Ayatollah Taleghani to run for president, but he said it is not in the interest of religious leaders to take part in the government; they should go back to Mosques. At the same time, the first ambassador that was appointed happened to be in the clergy.

New newspapers have started up, and political groups are distributing their publications.

Two groups of women invited the others to join them, regardless of their ideals, to work for equality of women and men. I do not believe in any of them.

Whatever we achieved in past years has vanished in an instant. Now it is their turn to build on the ruins.

JUNE 9, 1979

Yesterday it was announced that all the banks are going public. For two days, all the banks were closed until supervisors were assigned by the government. The object is the protection of people's savings, the adjustment of interest rates, and commissioning the industries. Most banks are on the verge of bankruptcy with the great loans they have given to industries. The managers ran away, and industries are almost stopped.

The Central Bank is in a shortage of skilled personnel; it is unlikely to be able to control other banks. The banking system will be the same as the government offices. God knows what will happen. So far the method of payment of compensation and management of banks is not clear.

At present, the internal situation of Khuzestan is peaceful. They reached an agreement with the opposition, which depends on the whether the constitution recognizes their autonomy or not. To avoid discussion about the constitution, it has been approved in a forty-member council, and there will be no Experts Council or making a referendum. Warnings and views expressed by the opposition were not heard.

A bill about newspapers has been approved that faced serious objection of writers. We do not know why we should have a bill about newspapers that involves limitations before having a constitution.

Nazih, president of the Lawyers Association and managing director of the Oil Company, had comments on the constitution and expressed them courageously.

While we have problems inside Iran, some

differences appear with Iraq. Iraq has bombarded some of the bordering cities of Iran. The root of differences is not clear. It is possible that it is about Iraqi Kurds that are demanding autonomy as Iranian Kurds.

It is said that the export of gas to Russia has been cut. The reaction is not yet clear. Some pipe-laying works have started to make busy people with jobs.

JUNE 12, 1979

Contrary to the claim of the equality of women, the government has refrained from accepting women for training in judicial jobs. Those who already passed the training are not being accepted for judiciary jobs. They take sanctuary in the Ministry of Justice.

Dr. Matindaftary, an active leader of the National Front, who was on a trip to Europe, has disappeared in the airport. Nobody explained his disappearance. Everything in Iran is becoming unusual. In the universities, they expel professors. In the Ministry of Foreign Affairs, two hundred diplomats were dismissed. They do not know how these dismissals damage the foreign policy. When an inexperienced physician, Dr. Velyati, was appointed as minister of Foreign Affairs, most of the diplomats preferred to be out of their jobs.

Banks have been made public and the presidents were elected; some of the ex-presidents remained, but their service locations were changed. Banking systems suffer from a shortage of specialists. The government stated that it will compensate the shareholders and people's deposits are guaranteed. If the result of change is not a reduction of interest rate and a just distribution of credit, people will not benefit from it. The danger for banks is the spread of bureaucratic spirit of the government among the Banks personnel. If there is no healthy competition between banks, the polite behavior of private banks with their customers will vanish. Banks became public when most of the deposits were taken out of the banks.

After the banks, insurance companies were made public. They are also trying to make the industries public and have submitted a plan in this regard to the Revolutionary Committee.

JUNE 24, 1979

On Friday, the first big protest on the decision of the government to put the Constitution on referendum took place. The demonstration was held by lawyers and the National Democratic Front, which was scattered by force. The pasdaran tore the slogans and cut their loudspeakers. They are objecting to seventy selected people: those who are supported by Ayatollah Khomeini and Ayatollah Shariatmadari. These leaders first spoke about a selective council, and then they reached to seventy selected members for the Experts Council.

There are riots in different provinces, news of which is censored. Some Kurds like to immigrate to neighboring countries. They claim that SAVAK, the Shah's friends, Iraq, and Kuwait are paying for the riots.

The minister of justice has resigned. Amirentezam, the government's speaker who never gave enough information to people, was assigned to the position of ambassador in Sweden. In the shuffle of the cabinet, no new minister entered. Hajseyedjavadi, the minister of the interior, holds the position of minister of justice as well. The Ministry of Justice is actually invalid. The Revolutionary Committee is regularly busy with investigations, detentions, and executions of people.

JULY 1, 1979

Life goes on as usual; people are depressed and disappointed. Unemployment among the young generation and the intellectuals is serious. Everybody is displeased about what they are doing, and there is no discipline at workplaces. There are some in strikes and protests without response. The government is weaker now. The religious duty that they have initiated has isolated people.

So far the method of the constitution approval is not clear, and no solution for resolving the problem is in sight.

Yesterday an armed group occupied Mehrabad Airport. They went on board a flight without showing a valid passport. One of them was the son of Ayatollah Montazeri. The government did not want to get involved and sat back.

While the government shows weakness, there are revolutionary courts that kill the opposition very quickly. In the constitutional government, they observe no right for the autonomy of different minorities that caused the riots in different cities.

The secret meeting between Ayatollah Khomeini, the Revolutionary Court, and the ministers was delayed due to security reasons. There are some disputes from Dr. Yazdi with the Islamic Republic Party and Khalkhali, who said that, "I am the only one who makes decisions." His statements were rejected; every day he makes some new problems. Once he tried to change the name of Persian Gulf to the Islamic Gulf, he granted some islands to Arab States, and then he threatened the leader of the Arabic-speaking tribes, Al Shabestari Khaghani. He also issued an order for the Shah's assassination. He said that he has hired Karlos, the international terrorist, to kill the Shah. Nobody knows exactly who he is. He claims to be the chief of Fadaeean Islam's prison, but the group denied this. Khalkhali takes part in the Revolutionary Courts and easily and quickly issues killing orders.

The Prime Minister (Bazargan) speaks of numerous decision making centers. Actually, the country is like a city with thousands of governors and everybody plays their own tune.

JULY 30, 1979

At last the Specialists Council has started, and a new movement has taken place. All of the groups introduced their candidates. By order of Ayatollah Khomeini, the religious groups became united and left no chance to the others. In the first Friday prayer, Ayatollah Taleghani stated that the opposition should have a chance, and different views should come forward. If they would not like to participate, he invited them to come. He said the media should be available to all groups. It seems that the original prefabricated text of the constitution will be approved with the majority of votes. Bazargan said that the minorities should speak by the size of their votes.

Kurdistan still has an internal war. War has become more serious in East and West Azerbaijan. People in Marivan moved collectively and spread out in the desert to show their protest. The army arrived, and people slept in front of tanks to stop their movement. Khuzestan became a very sensitive zone with trouble from outside and inside. The United States and European countries clearly started to disagree with the Islamic Republic of Iran. Disputes with Libya are not settled in the case of Imam Mousa Sadr (a Muslim imam killed in Libya). Now the only supporting country is Palestine.

It is a strange world. Even stranger is the behavior

of some supporters of the Islamic republic. In Germany, they have started a Revolutionary Court and accused some people of the crime of working with SAVAK and executed them. The case made Germans upset and expelled or detained some Iranians. Iranian authorities did not accept any responsibility in this case.

The Revolutionary Council works constantly; they even interfere with cases that are not revolutionary. They have executed a few prostitutes without a hearing. They convicted Dr. Sheikholeslamzadeh, the minister of health in different cabinets, and condemned him to a life sentence because they needed his service in the prisons.

In a TV interview, Ayatollah Khomeini declared that music is harmful for the society and is the same as opium. The statement made for a good topic for those outside of Iran. While TV has no acceptable programs, his statement about music was more disappointing. Gradually every venue is closed to the people, and they have to live in a huge prison. Instead of music, they put on air mourning marshes and Arabic songs. We are not allowed to hear our own national music.

Due to economic, social, and political problems, peace is not coming forward. Newspapers are full of terrible news from around the country. The government and Revolutionary Council are mixed. Nobody knows who they are, and every day they make new and hasty decisions then hide themselves.

AUGUST 12, 1979

Election of the Experts Council has happened and all members were elected among candidates of the Islamic Republic Party. They did not let one person with a different idea in the council. The result of the election was known ahead of time. This method is not in the interest of anybody. They could at least give an opportunity to a few others to make this election valid. Advertisements of other groups were torn and gatherings were scattered. They cover their mistakes and neglect the protests. Now they are going to have a parliament with uniform members.

Before the start of the Experts Council, they made a great attack on the newspaper *Ayandegan*. They sealed the machines and detained the editorial personnel. They attacked the workers and broke their strike by force. They said that the newspaper was working with Zionists. In view of a neutral reader, the newspaper was a very interesting one, and many intellectuals were writing articles for it. They stopped the other newspaper, *Ahangar*, a comic paper with very intelligent jokes, from printing in the same place. In fact, they have imprisoned freedom of speech and thought. Soon we shall hear no voice except that of the newspapers that are loud speakers of the Islamic Republic Party. Stoppage of newspapers will result in unawareness of the people.

Against the protests of writers, the Bill of Newspapers has been approved in the Revolutionary Council. This will result in hard pressure on newspapers and print houses.

Ayatollah Khomeini announced that every strike and reduction in work is an action against Islam and the revolution. This became an excuse for hard liners to stop every protest and deny this natural right of the people.

Bazargan's government has a weak status. The prime minister seems like a religious leader rather than a political leader. From the start of Ramadan, Friday prayers take place with Ayatollah Taleghani. The prayers are mostly political and have many participants. In the beginning, there were speeches to encourage unity among people. In the very hot summer time, many people participated in the prayer, which had great political impacts.

The construction of the Jihad in rural areas is going on but it can do very little. To provide housing for poor people, it is said that vacant houses will be given to them. The minister of housing denied this and said it needs a law. Maybe he is not aware of the current lawlessness.

AUGUST 14, 1979

Yesterday a big demonstration was organized by the National Democratic Party to protest the closure of *Ayadegan* and the other newspapers. The route was from Tehran University to the prime minister's office. It ended with a harsh attack of Hezbollah members that were armed with knives, stones, and fists. About three hundred people were wounded, and demonstrators were humiliated. In the prime minister's office, nobody cared for them. They could not even read their statement. The contact had a very negative impact on people. Because of the newspaper bill that was approved by the Revolutionary Council, newspapers are closing every day and many journalists are being detained. Apparently the protest is against the new writers of *Ayandegan* who have nothing to do with the previous writers. Censorship of newspapers will cause the riots in provinces to be hidden.

Yesterday, a meeting was arranged by Hezbollah to oppose *Ayandegan,* which was supported by the government. The leaders were marching in the street with clubs and making funny slogans. On their route, they looted bookstores that were selling leftist books. They called them the enemy and burned the leftist documents. Fadaeeyan Khalgh, of the left wing group, showed no resistance. This shows how they have broken with the party that had a very effective partnership with them in toppling the Shah.

They cleared their aim. Society is divided into the religious, nonreligious, left, right, and the Shah's supporters (Taghouti). This division will result in the failure of the revolution.

For whatever reason the people are standing against each other, that reason will weaken their front against the enemy. The prime minister looks at the events with a neutral stand and lets the events happen. Suffocation becomes tighter every day, and hope for a constitution that guarantees human rights diminishes.

SEPTEMBER 1, 1979

There are riots in Kurdistan, Paveh, and other cities. The army, gendarmerie, and Basij (partisans) are ready to attack the rioters. The leaders of the Democratic Party, Ezaldin Hosseini and Ghasemloo are getting help from outside of Iran, and they resist with their armed forces against the army. They are subject to Ayatollah Khomeini's anger, who is the chief commander.

Sadegh Khalkhali has started field courts in Kurdistan which are now trying and executing many. Mahabad is surrounded by the Democratic Party; army forces are only five kilometers from the city. Today three army helicopters were shot.

Ayatollah Khomeini made some mitigation for newspapers and ordered the public prosecutor to investigate their cases. It is expected that some newspapers will start again, provided that they do not write against the Islamic republic. At the moment, only a few newspapers are published with great consciousness.

Foreign media is not secure in the Islamic republic, and some reporters are deported. The radio and TV, as usual, are not giving the correct news. As of today, Iran joined the Conference of Non-Alliance Countries. Dr. Yazdi, the minister of foreign affairs, announced that Iran is not a signatory to any defense agreements and has cancelled agreements with Socialist countries.

SEPTEMBER 5, 1979

Yesterday, army and Pasdaran troops entered Mahabad and Baneh, the stations of the Kurds. All people, even leaders of the riots, are given immunity if they hand over their arms. Some leaders already escaped, and some people fled to the mountains. Cities are experiencing a shortage of food and oil. Ayatollah Khomeini ordered the government to take serious steps in the development of Kurdistan. It is decided that one day of oil income is assigned to each province.

Foreign reporters have limitations. The Associated Press office in Tehran is closed. The newspapers that were closed are still not opened. Newspaper stands have no customers.

SEPTEMBER 15, 1979

A great loss has happened to Iranian society. The great revolutionary man, Ayatollah Taleghani, passed away suddenly in front of thousands of followers after a very courageous speech in Friday prayer. He was a very valuable personality for the regime. He spent many years in detention, and managed to solve problems with patience and love. People loved him and respected his views; he was away from religious prejudice and respected minorities' rights and worked for them. He hated harshness. He believed in people and emphasized people's participation. He had a majority in the Experts Council but had little influence. His life came to a dead end. There were plenty of demands, and he had no facilities.

Three days of mourning with great respect were held for him. People were crying as if they had lost a lovable father. No religious leader holds his position among people to replace the empty space.

OCTOBER 10, 1979

The situation in Kurdistan is terrible. Yesterday, fifty Pasdars were killed, and some were taken hostage. Harsh behavior from both parties made for a very miserable environment. More harshness is expected. They break gas and oil pipes. Every day Partisan groups create some events; they blew up a passenger train resulting in the killing of sixty-five people. Nazih, the managing director of the Oil Company was dismissed by Ayatollah Ghodousi's accusations. It was hard for people to see what happened to a person who was supported by the prime minster and worked hard for the revolution.

The markets for foreign newspapers and radios are very hot. To find the truth, people look for them. Through this media, people realized that the government made an agreement with the United States to purchase spare parts for arms and in turn sell them oil. However, in the general meeting of the United Nations, Dr. Ebrahim Yazdi said that the relationship between Iran and the United States is cold.

Oriana Fallaci, a famous Italian journalist, had a very controversial interview with Ayatollah Khomeini that was published in the Iranian press after being censored. This woman journalist heard and published whatever she wanted; she spoke of the treatment of women, suffocation, dictatorship, trials, and the unpleasant political environment for women. The interview was a surprise for the world media. Oriana Fallaci could make Ayatollah so angry that he revealed his inner thoughts, especially on the matters of dictatorship and women.

The Experts Council approved the constitution that gives no opportunity to the people. Clergies, Velayat Faghih (the full authority of the leader), and the Guardian Council have full authority. No privilege is foreseen for the minorities. As long as censorship is practiced, we cannot hear any protests.

The Bazargan cabinet was shuffled. This time, Chamran, a doubtful personality, became the minister of defense. It is possible that the prime minister trusts him, but in the view of the people, he was far from the country and his way of life was not well known.

OCTOBER 30, 1979

Students organized a demonstration that demanded free political debates and protested the high tuitions. Some people attacked them with knives and made them quiet.

Today women demonstrated and protested against the cancellation of the Family Protection Law. Ayatollah Khomeini said that women can obtain the right to divorce at the time of marriage. It is not clear what would be the situation of women who married before this law.

Even the very conservative newspapers started to complain. The minister of health resigned and reasoned that the cabinet is not strong enough. He wrote a very harsh letter to Ayatollah and the prime minister. It is possible that some more changes happened in the cabinet that could not solve the problems.

The meeting for review of the constitution did not care about protests by the people and approved a terrible text that limited all individual freedoms. Everything is in the hands of clergies, Velayat Faghih, and the Guardian Council, even appointment and dismissal of the president.

With the wisdom and intelligence of the Iranian people, the clergies should now decide for themselves. They say Iran is part of the Islamic territory, and they deem themselves to defend the Islamic territories, which is very controversial.

There is a rumor about millions of dollars that were misused in the Ministry of Commerce while helping some clergies of the Revolutionary Court. A public prosecutor has resigned his job and has had a very hard stand against the regime. It is clear that big corruption has happened. The prime minister was aware of it and ordered the Investigating Organization to work on it. Three ministers are also involved in the case. They are trying to attribute the food shortage to this incident.

The Shah has been hospitalized at Corner Hospital in New York due to spleen cancer. He received an unlimited residency permit. Some think that this is an excuse for the protection of the Shah. In London, there were demonstrations against the new regime of Iran; a few people were arrested and then released.

Moinfar, the new oil minister and previously the managing director of the Planning Organization, is famous for being mean. He had a very bad experience in the meeting with the Oil Company staff. He was badly beaten, and then stayed at home, claiming to be sick.

When people heard about shortage of oil production, they started to store oil and food.

NOVEMBER 6, 1979

It has been two days since the followers of Ayatollah Khomeini have occupied the U.S. embassy, sixty of the staff were taken hostage, and they confiscated the properties of the embassy. All of the clergies and Ayatollah Khomeini supported the occupation. They asked for surrender of the Shah and Farah. In a hasty interview, Ebrahim Yazdi called the hostage-taking a normal reaction of people and revealed the serious notices that were given to the United States in regard to the residency permit given to the Shah.

In the meantime, Bazargan, the prime minister, was undergoing criticism for negotiations in Algeria with Berjinesky, the former minister of foreign affairs in the United States. Now he has gone undercover.

The city is in chaos. People are making demonstrations and marching in front of the occupied embassy. The embassy of the United Kingdom was also occupied by the group that called themselves Followers of the Imam's Line. The UK embassy was later set free.

U.S. radio said that they will not surrender the Shah and recognized that the government of Iran is responsible for the lives of the hostages. The reaction to the hostage-taking is worldwide and has caused worry for many countries. It is possible that this crisis will last a long time.

The staff of the Oil Company said that they will stop the export of oil to the United States if that is the wish of Ayatollah Khomeini. So far, such an order is not issued.

One more minister resigned due to a lack of coordination and decisiveness by the cabinet. The government is in big trouble. From one side, they cannot resist the wish of Ayatollah Khomeini and his son

Ahmad; from the other side, there is international law and immunity of the embassy's staff, along with worry about reciprocate treatment from the United States. So far, no escape is in view. It is possible that a big change will happen in the cabinet.

The problems of Kurdistan have not been solved. Dariush Forouhar went to Kurdistan to negotiate about their claims. Every day, ordinary people, soldiers, and revolutionary guards are killed. There is no proper news about the region's situation. Some cities in Kurdistan are in the hands of the Democratic Party. There is no doubt that if privileges are given to people in Kurdistan, they have to be given to the other groups.

Every day a new problem appears, and the situation is getting more complicated.

NOVEMBER 10, 1979

Six days have passed since the hostages were taken, and no improvement has happened. Every day it gets more complicated. The Shah said that he is ready to leave the United States, but his condition is not fit for transfer. Ayatollah Khomeini did not agree to any intermediation. Representatives sent by President Carter stayed in Turkey. Every day a river of supporting students is pouring onto the TV screen.

Americans stopped flights of Iran Air to the United States and stopped selling spare parts for army equipments. Americans are not proceeding on any unusual action; they are afraid that they may endanger the safety of the hostages. The students started to reveal the contents of secret documents in the embassy.

Bazargan resigned. So far no order was issued with regard to the stoppage of oil sale to the United States. At present, the Revolutionary Council is running the country. Ministers were reinstated, except Dr. Ebrahim Yazdi. Banisadr became a member of the Revolutionary Council and the minister of foreign affairs. A wide advertisement campaign is started. All are watching Iran and want to know the end. The intermediation of the pope and Palestine Freedom Movement did not work.

The problem of Kurdistan is still not solved. Representatives of Bazargan were told to continue their works. In his last presentation, Bazargan provided revelations that were not allowed to be published. The National Front suggested the creation of a National Unity Government by all groups. However, the situation is so complicated that no acceptable result could be reached.

NOVEMBER 13, 1979

Ten days have passed since the hostages were taken. Every day the situation gets worse. The Revolutionary Court issued orders that oil to the United States be cut. Americans decided to expel Iranian students and prohibited the issuing of visas to Iranians. In the United States, demonstrations are going on; so far, one Iranian and one American were killed.

In Tehran, foreign embassies closed their doors to avoid similar incidents. German nationals left Iran. Airlines and vessels that were carrying goods for Iran are facing trouble. Banisadr, the newly appointed foreign minister, stated that he will not accept any proposal from the United States.

Ayatollah Khomeini only agreed to meet with a representative from the pope to receive the message from him. In his negotiations with the pope's representative, he complained that they are not thinking about the poor people of the world. He also asked the pope to put a religious duty on President Carter about the return of the Shah to Iran.

Economic pressure from the United States has accelerated. They promised not to stop the export of wheat, but they did so against the stop of oil exporting. Countries like Australia and Canada, who are friends of the United States, will not help Iran.

The Good Will Committee returned from Kurdistan and submitted their report to the Revolutionary Court, but the court did not make any comments in this regard and the crisis continues.

Sabaghian, the minister of state who performed good services for the revolution, such as the hasty and disgraceful election of city councils, was dismissed from the Ministry of State. A clergy member of the Revolutionary Court, Hashemi Rafsanjani, a close friend of Ayatollah Khomeini, became the minister of state at the time of the constitution referendum, election of the president, Parliament election, and City Council election.

Students that are stationed in the U.S. embassy make new disclosures every day about American friends, and every day there are support demonstrations in front of the embassy. At this time, the two parties are at a dead end. The prestige of President Carter depends on solving the hostage problem. He is avoiding harsh action so that no harm will come to the hostages.

Ayatollah Khomeini has cancelled his visits for two weeks. The Palestine Freedom Front said that they agree with fighting but not with this type of fight. Ayatollah Khomeini explicitly said that he does not let anybody, even Yasser Arafat, interfere with this issue. He will be ready to negotiate if the Shah is returned to Iran. With regard to the public opinion in United States, this is a difficult condition.

NOVEMBER 19. 1979

By order of Ayatollah Khomeini, thirteen women hostages and the black people who were not accused of spying were released.

Ayatollah Khomeini issued a statement with regard to accepting the wishes of the Kurds that was welcomed by them, and they continued their negotiations. So far the contents of the wishes have not been disclosed. It is possible that they are given some autonomy.

Pasdaran (guardians) are supposed to begin construction work in the region. That means they have nothing to do with security in the region.

The spirit of anti-imperialism is vivid, and at present, every other matter is in the shadow. Purchase of oil from Iran has been banned by the United States. They do not want to put Iran on sanction. Germany confirmed the U.S. policy regarding no purchase of oil and closing Iran's deposits. It is likely that they will do the same.

NOVEMBER 24, 1979

Everybody is waiting for war and attack by the United States. Hostage-taking in Iran was copied by Pakistan and Saudi Arabia. In Pakistan, four people were killed and two hundred were taken hostage for the occupation of Masjid Alharam. Iran stated that it is not paying back its foreign loans of fifteen billion dollars. European countries are in harmony with the United States in condemning Iran.

Once more, the situation in Kurdistan is in crisis, and the Good Will Committee returned to Tehran.

Detainees in Mashad prison created a riot, and four hundred of them escaped the prison.

U.S. marines are moving toward the Persian Gulf. In the United Sates, pressure and maltreatment of Iranian students continues. In Iran, demonstrations against the United States continue. In the Friday prayer, Ayatollah Montazeri humiliated the Kurdish leaders. We do not know what will be the effects of such behavior. Muslims are stimulated against the United States. U.S. Congress proposed harsh action against Iran. The Shah stated that he will leave the United States in two weeks' time. We do not know what is going to happen in two weeks. Students that are part of Followers of Imam's Line said they will kill hostages if the Shah is released from the United States.

NOVEMBER 26, 1979

Fighting between Iran and the United States is in full force. Every day there are demonstrations of different groups, and they call the U.S. embassy a "spy's nest."

The United States tries to show that it has nothing to do with the riots in front of Masjid Alharam, but Ayatollah Khomeini emphasized that the incident was done by Americans to ruin Islam and Muslims. He encouraged people in their demonstrations. A meeting of the Security Council is going to be held, but Iran will not participate because an unfavorable atmosphere against Iran is being created in the United States. People expect the foreign minister to proceed on negotiations. Banisadr, the foreign minister, refrains from taking part in the meeting because he knows that the students would not agree with him. An American senator, Hans, came to Iran to find a solution on his own initiative. He went through a very humiliating interview and then he visited the hostages. McBride, a representative from UNESCO and winner of the Nobel Peace Prize, came to Iran to find a friendly solution.

The Islamic Association proposed a council with seven members: three from Iran, three from the United States, and the secretary general of the United Nations. None of the proposals were accepted by the students; they are not satisfied with any solution except the return of the Shah.

In Kurdistan, a twenty-day ceasefire was announced. Statements by Ayatollah Montazeri about the Kurdish leaders were about to start a new fire. They solved the problem quickly and said that the comments were his personal views.

In a conference supported by some groups, women asked for the equality of rights, cancellation of unilateral divorce, and the stoppage of job discrimination against women. They also asked for military training, a review of the cancellation of the Family Protection Law, and an increase in the legal marriage age which had been lowered by the clergies.

DECEMBER 1, 1979

It was decided that on December 11 and 12; the constitution will be forwarded for referendum. Many groups have banned participation. The critical points are Velayat Faghih and autonomy of minorities. Ayatollah Khomeini religiously bound people to take part in the referendum and promised to add the faults to the amendment.

Bani Sadr was dismissed from the Ministry of Foreign Affairs, and Sadegh Ghotbzadeh, the nutty boy of the revolution, was appointed to the job. He announced that he will not take part in the Security

Council for judgments on the Iran–America case. Ayatollah Khomeini said he will not agree with the judgments of the Security Council no matter what it is.

The Mexican government refused to give a visa to the Shah. Anvarsadat, the president of Egypt, announced his readiness for having Shah. He will be a great headache. The Shah said he may go to the Bahamas.

The Student Followers of Imam's Line said they will put the hostages on trial with the accusation of spying. President Carter said he will not bear the trial of the hostages, and that would be considered declaring war.

On Ashura and Tasoua (religious mourning days), demonstrations were high. In other countries, some demonstrations were held in favor of Ayatollah Khomeini. Students in the United States are having a terrible time; they are intimidated by people and the government has closed the accounts of Iranians in the U.S. banks. There is no means for sending them money. The United States claims that it will not impose economic pressure on Iran; however, on borders the workers refrain from loading ships going to Iran. The United States complained about Iran to the League's International Court, and its meeting will be held this week. Three members of the Revolutionary Court are going to France to explain Iran's situation.

Many countries support Iran with regard to the interference of the United States and crimes by the Shah, but they cannot justify taking hostages. People in Iran are passing their days with great worry, and each day the knot becomes more twisted. We cannot foresee what will happen.

DECEMBER 4, 1979

It was decided that on the anniversary of the regime change, February 11, the election of Parliament and the president will happen. The result can be anticipated ahead of time.

The Security Council has suggested that Iran and the United States solve their problems in the League's International Court, and Iran release the hostages immediately. Today, Ghotbzadeh announced that the hostages will definitely go on trial.

In a military hospital in Texas, the Shah is hospitalized for rehabilitation, and his next destination is not clear. More so than the first days, people in the United States have sympathy for the Shah.

Iran proposed to the OPEC conference of foreign ministers that they receive the oil money in another currency consisting of several valid international currencies. The dollar is going down in the world markets. Election competition for the presidency has started in the United States; every candidate tries to take advantage of the events in Iran. Ted Kennedy made a very harsh speech against the Shah and supported the people in Iran. President Carter claims that with his soft contact, he prevented a crisis.

DECEMBER 9, 1979

In Tabriz, the referendum for the constitution ended in catastrophe. Ayatollah Kazem Shariatmadari, a religious leader, defined his views on the constitution. The text has been read on TV by Sadegh Shariatmadari, and a picture of Kazem Shariatmadari was on the screen. As a result, people of Tabriz voted yes for the constitution. Partners of Ayatollah Shariatmadari found out about the cheating, and they attacked government buildings and occupied radio and TV stations and the office of the governor. The air force joined them in a huge riot. In West Azerbaijan, the same happened. In Ghom, a group of people attacked the home of Ayatollah Shariatmadari; two guards were killed. Now Tabriz and Oroumieh are out of the government's control. Ayatollah Khomeini made a visit to Ayatollah Shariatmadari to solve the problem. A committee chaired by Bazargan went to Tabriz. In a TV message, Bazargan said that foreigners are involved in this incident. That made people upset and they refrained from negotiation.

Sistan and Bluchistan demand autonomy. They gave one week for a response; otherwise they will be armed and enter a war.

The central government is facing a big problem. The United States makes its sanction tighter and confiscated assets of Iran. The insurance rate in the Persian Gulf as a war zone has increased four times and loading vessels has become more difficult.

Student Followers of Imam's Line disclose new documents every day to show that the American diplomats were spies. Ghotbzadeh said he will not go to the League's International Court.

Shahram, the son of Asharaf Pahlavi, the Shah's sister, was assassinated in Paris. Khalkhali said that it was done by Fadaeean Islam. The Forghan group accepted responsibility.

Some documents were found in the U.S. Embassy against Rahmatollah Maraghee, the chair of the Khalgh Moslman Party. He was prosecuted, and his assets were confiscated.

People in Tabriz do not care for TV messages by Ayatollah Shariatmadari. Their main protests are about the article on Velayat Faghih, the lack of autonomy for minorities, and the city councils not being properly defined. However, some people voted yes to the constitution.

The problem of Azerbaijan is getting complicated, especially when the Kurds declared their coordination with them.

Now every media source in the world has discussions about Iran. Some Iranian youths decided to join Mohammad Montazeri and go to Lebanon to fight with Israel. The matter was faced by Lebanon with fury, and they said they will not let Iranians interfere in Lebanon. They changed their minds.

DECEMBER 17, 1979

Due to riots in Azerbaijan, Ayatollah Shariatmadari announced that he will not interview with foreign journalists. Upon pressure by the clergies, the Khalgh-e Mosalman Party closed its branches and their newsletter was banned. At present, a committee of government authorities is negotiating. Six thousand people from Ardabil resigned from the Khalgh-e Mosalman Party. A dispute between the two clergies ended up in favor of Ayatollah Khomeini.

The Shah has gone to Panama from the United States. The Revolutionary Court said that they consider the United States responsible for the Shah's surrender. A big international jury will investigate crimes and interferences of the United States in Iran. Ghotbzadeh said that trial of the hostages is changed to a trial of the United States. This court should be something like the Nuremberg Court. It will happen in the New Year, meaning in two weeks.

Hostages were given the right of visitations for the New Year, and they can have their own ceremony.

The elections of the president and Parliament have been delayed for one month.

Iran and OPEC countries raised the oil price.

The pressure on Iranian students in the United States is accelerating, and they are in a financial shortage. They are being expelled using different excuses. High IQ students may request political asylums. Money sent from Iran for the students is not being handed to them. A number of youths are in great stress over this inhumane treatment.

As it was expected, the League's International Court ruled for the freeing of the hostages. The United States forwarded the decision to the Security Council and asked for the economic sanction of Iran.

The departure of the Shah from the United States made no change in the situation. So far, the United States has not decided about a return of the Shah's assets. Iran may take legal action and forward the claims to the U.S. courts. Authorities in Iran's foreign affairs are busy compiling the documents.

JANUARY 3, 1979

At last the United States forwarded the verdict of the League's International Court to the Security Council and asked for economic punishment of Iran. The Security Council gave Iran one week and assigned Kurt Waldheim (the former secretary general of the United Nations) to negotiations with Iran. His entry into Iran caused great demonstrations. Ghotbzadeh said that he will not negotiate with Waldheim on the hostages. He only saw crimes of the United States and the Shah. If in one week's time a solution is not reached for freedom of the hostages, the resolution about economic sanction against Iran will be discussed in the Security Council.

Interference of Russia in Afghanistan surpassed the problem of Iran that was protested by all countries, including Iran. At the moment, Iran is fighting on two fronts, right and left against the United States and Russia. What Russia has done is strange because Babrak Karmal had the full support of them when he started to run Afghanistan.

January 7, 1980

Waldheim left Iran, and his mission had failed. In Iran, an assassination was attempted against him. He submitted his report to the Security Council and asked the economic sanction to be delayed.

The Shah expressed his readiness for trial in an international court, provided that neutral persons run the trial. It did not work, and Ayatollah Khomeini still requests return of the Shah.

There are riots in different cities, especially at the ports. In Lengeh Port, twenty-eight people were killed in the riot. In Tabriz, some club holders made trouble for people.

Radio and TV have changed many hands. In Kurdistan, a struggle happened between the local people and the mission from Tehran. They ask for the dismissal of the Pasdaran. The minister of the interior said they will be there until discipline rules.

The war in Afghanistan had hard effects on the relationship between Iran and Russia. It is decided that the matter will go to the Security Council. So far some countries have started a sanction against Russia.

JANUARY 15, 1980

Now people are busy with election of the president. Ayatollah Khomeini did not use his power as Velayat Faghih in the election and gave the right to people. At the beginning, the number of candidates was 104. They said it is an American conspiracy to make Iran's election invalid because some illiterate and some unknown people participated in the election. Hojatoleslam Khoini was responsible for interviewing the candidates. He did not let them use the media for propaganda.

The Islamic Republic Party introduced Jalalaldin Farsi as a candidate. Then it was disclosed that his Iranian origin is doubtful, and he was rejected. Only about seven or eight people who are close friends of Ayatollah Khomeini are producing propaganda. The best chances lie with Banisadr and Madani, then Habibi, Ghatbzadeh, and Tabatabaei. Clergies were prohibited to join the election.

After the election of president and the cabinet formation, the parliament election will take place. It is possible that with less decision-making bodies, we can be more at peace.

A resolution by the United States about economic sanction of Iran has been vetoed by Russia; as a result, the United States announced that it will enforce the resolution with other countries. Eight countries gave a positive vote to the resolution. China did not participate, and East Germany and Russia voted against it. Occupation of Afghanistan by Russia has under-shadowed Iran's problem.

The reelection of Indira Gandhi in India, who is supported by Russia, has caused imbalance among the powers in the region. The United States has given Pakistan four hundred million dollars in military aid to resist a possible attack by Russia. The Russian ambassador to Mexico quoted Ayatollah Khomeini saying, "To settle riots in Iran, I will seek help from Russia." It was later denied.

There are riots in all provinces, such as Azerbaijan, Kurdistan, Isfahan, and Kerman. The head of the special mission to Kurdistan said it is the last time he goes there. They try not to talk about Tabriz. At present, Ayatollah Shariatmadari lives in Ghom and announced that he will have nothing to do with the Jomhoury Khalgh-e Moslaman Party. Its branches are halted everywhere.

A few members of the Forghan Group that were responsible for the murder of a few clergies are being detained. The Pasdaran announced that they have not finished their job; they may return and kill some more people.

JANUARY 24, 1980

Tomorrow is the election day of the first Islamic republic president. Hot pre-election days have passed. Disclosing and propaganda was at a high. Farsi, the candidate of Islamic Republic Party, was rejected because his parents were Afghan. Some others were rejected from the start because they were cooperating with the Shah's regime. Two clergies, Rafsanjani and Beheshti, did not participate by order of Ayatollah Khomeini. They were attacked by another clergy named Tehrani. Election of the president caused a crack in the line of clergies. Even when the election is over, they will not have the unity they had at the beginning.

Yesterday, Ghotbzadeh announced that the president of Panama arrested the Shah and it caused some excitement. Later it was denied by different news agencies. Maybe it was a trick to attract more votes for the president.

The United States has delayed the sanctions against Iran and asked negotiations to be carried on. The secretary general of the United Nations stated that he is in the process of forming a committee to investigate the Shah's wrongdoings and the claims of Iran against the United States. He expects the hostages will be released as soon as the committee is held. Ghotbzadeh said the hostages will be released when the decision of this committee is announced. Surely the work of such a committee will be complicated and long. In case the release of the hostages depends on the announcement of the committee's decision, they should take it easy and come to the end in a short time.

The occupation of Afghanistan by Russia has wide repercussions in the world and may cause the start of a third world war. Now the position of countries on this issue is clear. The Palestine Freedom Party is supporting Russia, and Iran is against Russia and supports Muslims in Afghanistan.

After the revolution, Iran and the Palestine Freedom Party were very close friends and they knew every detail about Iran. Many of the government authorities are in close relationship with them.

Today it was announced that Ayatollah Khomeini will be transferred from Ghom to Heart Hospital in Tehran, but it has been repeatedly announced that he is alright. It seems he suffered from a heart attack; with the pressures he faced recently, it seems possible. These are days so close to reaching his great wish (an Islamic republic). At the present time, he is the only hope of many people, but with disputes among clergies, we cannot hope for the sustaining of the situation.

One candidate for presidency was Massoud Rajavi, the leader of Mojahedin Khalgh that was rejected by the order of Ayatollah Khomeini because he did not vote for the constitution. That disappointed his followers and the Kurds that were about to vote for him.

Upon request of the Sunnis, Ayatollah Khomeini promised to revise the article in the constitution about the official religion of the state. In the regions where the majority are Sunni, their official religion will be Sunni. This made Sunnites at Sistan and Balouchestan happy. As a result, they participated in the election of the president, which was banned by them. An alarm is given for election days; they expect some riots.

A National Iranian airline, HOMA, hit the mountains on the way from Mashad to Tehran, and 120 people were killed. There are plenty of rumors about this accident, and it is under investigation.

JANUARY 27, 1980

The first presidency election of the Islamic Republic of Iran was held on Friday, January 25, 1980. There were some worries about possible corruption, but nothing happened. It went peacefully and Abulhassan Banisadr was elected with a good majority. In his pre-election statements, he emphasized democracy and avoiding force and also improvement of the economic situation of the country. Upon Islamic concepts, he preached economic ideas. One that was supported by the people was the reduction of interest rates and the guarantee of people's deposits. He reduced the interest rates on housing and agriculture loans to 4 percent and promised to pay the balance from the state budget.

Since Banisadr gained 70 percent of the votes, there will be no need for a second round of voting. Second in the list was Madani. In the beginning, he made wide propaganda, and it was possible to win the election. But some corruption occurred which resulted in the reduction of his votes. Students disclosed a statement that showed one of his colleagues had contact with the United States embassy, which had no substance, but it resulted in his loss. Ayatollah Khomeini asked the candidates to cooperate with the elected president and all did so, excluding Madani.

Some physicians were called from Switzerland to look after Ayatollah Khomeini. They say he is well. His physical situation does not let him manage the country. After him, there is nobody that can maintain the unity of the country and be acceptable by a majority. The president can not start his job before a Parliament election. At present, the Revolutionary Council is running the country.

Muslim countries have held a conference in Islamabad to protest the Russian occupation of Afghanistan. Iran has taken part in the conference. Student Followers of Imam's Line have condemned the conference and called it a conspiracy by the United States. The Revolutionary Council deemed participation in the conference a must. These students deem themselves runners of the country and interfere in every matter. The president stated that he will solve the problem of the hostages.

The Iranian government is busy compiling documents against the Shah to present to the Panama Court, and is requesting the return of the Shah. Sixty days was given for this issue. During this period, the Shah will be under the supervision of the Panama government but not in prison.

FEBRUARY 10, 1980

The president started his work. He will shuffle the cabinet. It is decided that the Revolutionary Council will continue its job until Parliament is elected. The president is chair of the Revolutionary Council. The election will start about March 6. Candidates have one week to present themselves. The president will be responsible for running an appropriate election. On the occasion of fifteenth century of Hijrat (the Muslim calendar) and the change of government to the Islamic republic, celebrations were held and 240 guests were invited by the responsible committee and the Student Followers of Imam's Line.

Due to problems occurring during broadcasting of the swearing-in ceremony of the president, the supervisor of TV and Radio, who is the leader of the Student Followers of Imam's Line, had to resign. From now on, the Revolutionary Court will supervise this organization. The TV and Radio Organization is one of the most problematic organizations. The organization is divided in two groups. The programs are not educational, entertaining, or giving news. It is totally at the hands of the Student Followers of Imam's Line, and every day they make new chaos by making statements against somebody. The last of which was about the minister of national guidance, Naser Minachi. He was arrested for forty-eight hours and released by order of the president. In this regard, Mehdi Bazargan, the prime minister, elaborated that the matter was not something new; contact with the United States was related to the Shah's time. Minachi did not deny his contact.

It was decided that disclosing meetings with the U.S. be conditional and the documents given to

Revolutionary Court. They will be disclosed when the public prosecutor deems it appropriate.

The International Committee for investigation of the Shah's actions will be held shortly. They are expecting to receive the documents that are to be compiled by the Iranian government.

Ayatollah Khomeini has recovered. Doctors recommended him staying at the hospital for a longer time to pass a rehabilitation period. They brought him to the balcony of the hospital to be seen by the guests, and he managed to talk with them. It seems that the president has control over the country, and decision-making centers are getting in shape.

FEBRUARY 23, 1980

Banisadr is working hard against the obstacles in his way. He is standing firm, including on the chaos in Gonbbad. He is constantly talking with people and is not scared to tell about his problems. He has condemned any kind of strike. He said his eyes and ears are open to those who have complaints. He is ready to solve the problems in a friendly manner.

Two days ago, the gathering at Tehran University turned ugly and a few were wounded. The objective of the gathering was a protest against the method of carrying the election that is expected in two weeks' time. The Ministry of the Interior announced two stages of the election; that is not acceptable to many, and it is under reasoning that it is not compatible with the constitution. They also protested the candidacy of the minister of the interior and some other authorities that are going to use the government facilities in their own favor.

Ayatollah Khomeini has almost recovered. He

reduced his decision-making power by delegating his authorities to the president and the elected Guardian Council.

Today the delegation of the United Nations for investigation into the Shah's crimes come to Tehran. There is no clear promise on the release of the fifty American. Although it was told that the students should deliver the documents to the Revolutionary Court, they still do their disclosing through the help of Radio and Television that is under their control.

Banisadr asked the United States to confess to their crimes in Iran and to stop interfering in Iran and make no obstacle in the way of the Investigation Committee. President Carter did not confess to wrongdoings and interfering in Iranian affairs. Therefore, no progress has happened in the hostage situation.

In Tehran, a three-day national mobilization was declared. These days, private cars cannot come to the city centre to prevent the heavy air pollution. Also, it is a measure to make people prepare for the hardship that is on the way. So far, high prices, shortage of food, and unemployment are big problems. To solve unemployment, they have taken some steps and assigned some budget for it.

APRIL 7, 1980

During the time that these notes were not written, no progress has happened. Every day the situation of the country becomes worse. The election had many faults and wrongdoings. Those in power were elected. Complaints are many. One month's time is given to investigate them, and then a second election will be implemented. So, there will be no Parliament for two months.

The Shah has gone to Egypt from Panama and undergone surgery for his cancer. No change is made in the situation of the American hostages. America agreed to stop sanctions for the time being if they release the hostages. The Revolutionary Council and office of Ayatollah Khomeini implicitly opposed the proposal. Therefore, as of today, economical and political sanction of Iran by the United States and the Allies will start.

There is internal crisis in Kurdistan, Khuzestan, and the bordering cities. Every day they blow up oil pipes. Recently, Kermanshah Refinery was hit by a bomb. They believe the Iraqis are behind the bombings. The relationship between Iran and Iraq is disturbed. Iraqis claim that Iran should evacuate the three islands, Great and Little Tombs and Abumousa, and give them to Iraq. They are important from a strategic view point. Every day they expel the Shiites from Iraq and leave them in Iranian borders. It is said that Iranian Generals and SAVAK staff that escaped from Iran are living in Iraq. Banisadr has many headaches; most importantly, incompatibility with the Revolutionary Court.

High prices, unemployment, and lack of security are high. At the same time, the political problems with the United States are getting more complicated, and there is no hope of release.

APRIL 10, 1980

Iran and the United States cut their economic and political ties. The United States prohibited any export, even food and pharmaceuticals, to Iran. They declared that they will pay compensation to the hostage's families and the private and public entities from the nine billion dollars in seized Iranian bank deposits, and they will block Iranian ship routes at sea.

Ayatollah Khomeini said, "Cutting the relationship with the United States is a good omen. America is disappointed with Iran." Banisadr calls economical sanction preliminary to economic independence and release from rule by imperialists. He called for a demonstration on Friday. All Iranian diplomats were expelled from the United States. It is expected that thousands of Iranian students are expelled as well.

Iraq continues its troublemaking. So far, more than sixteen thousand Iranians were expelled from Iraq and sent to Iranian borders. Iraqi airplanes violate Iranian air borders. Iraq is supported by the United States. Apparently, in Iran they are not taking this seriously, while all news agencies in the world are discussing it.

Western European countries have not followed the American pattern. They are waiting for a common decision in all European countries. Italy refrained from delivery of spare parts for the purchased helicopters. Due to many explosions in oil pipes, production has reduced. The minister of oil said they are not going to sell oil to countries that participate in sanctions. It seems that with the closing of Hormoz Strait, the sale of oil would be difficult. The president said that we face no shortage. This kind of statement has internal use.

It is possible that President Carter is doing something to release the hostages, because this would affect his election. Every day we are expecting new problems. Now, the many involvements between Iran and the United States are showing up, to the extent that even telephone calls become difficult. If European countries join the sanction, it would make sending money for students in the United States more difficult, and many of them are compelled to come back home. In such a situation, they will have no job and no opportunity for continuing their education. In an unstable environment, it is hard to foresee anything.

Four out of five members of the committee for investigation of the election votes have resigned from the job. With many wrongdoings in the election, they forced it to be acceptable. The second round will be the same.

APRIL 20, 1980

Sanctions by the United States, Japan, and Western Europe become more serious every day. The United States speaks about planting mines in Iranian shores and making a military attack. Iran has not taken that seriously and says it will confront it.

In the middle of that trouble, the Islamic Association occupied universities and asked the political groups to evacuate the universities and take their offices away. The decision made leftist groups upset and fighting started. As a result, one person was killed and a great number were injured. Islamists claim that universities are not Islamic; they should change to Islamic standards. Examination time is close, and it is not clear what will happen. At the moment, the students are scattered in different cities. They are worried and upset. It is possible that the crisis will reach to the schools.

Fighting in Kurdistan has become serious; they resist against the army. Looking after borders is an excuse for suppression of the people in Kurdistan. Every day we hear about murder, destruction, and armed fights. The cities in Kurdistan are out of control. Banisadr is facing many problems. Like Bazargan, he complains about numerous decision-making bodies. Student Followers of Imam's Line intervene in every matter. So far, the American hostages are at their disposal. Unrest in the university started first at the University of Tabriz.

Rafsanjani went to Tabriz to make a speech; he was protested and his speech was interrupted. Then the Student Followers of Imam's Line occupied the university and expelled the students and professors. The same pattern was carried out in other universities. Protection of universities is given to the Revolutionary Guards and committees.

APRIL 22, 1980

The universities crisis has accelerated and resulted in many murders and injured. At last, all political groups are evacuated from the universities. The Islamic Association said they will not attend classes. Every university should be dissolved and start working with Islamic standards. A demonstration at Ayatollah Khomeini's residence was organized for this purpose. He confirmed that university's programs are not Islamic. It was decided that classes are cancelled. It seems that the universities will not be at peace in the near future. They said the examinations should finish soon, and the universities are closed. No university is ready for early examinations. It is decided that new programs are prepared for the universities, in a way that the country is free from the influence of imperialism.

European countries and Japan joined in the U.S. sanction. It was decided to minimize their trade with Iran, not issue visas for Iranians, not purchase oil, and not deliver spare parts. They have given two weeks' time to Iran to release the hostages. In case Iran does not comply with the conditions, they will make harder sanctions. Now Iran tries to get the spare parts from

Eastern Europe counties. In such a case, the result is that we are under control of communist countries and that would not be any good.

Yesterday there was a rumor that the president has resigned. He denied the rumor in a TV interview. All together it is a terrible situation, and it is not clear what would be at the end. Every day there is a new problem. Iran hopes that European countries do not all join the sanction, but England and Germany have had a harder stand.

APRIL 27, 1980

A strange event happened. The United States failed in an attempt to rescue the hostages. As a result, they lost one C130 airplane, six helicopters, and eight personnel. President Carter personally accepted the responsibility for the failure. They wanted to spread sleeping powder and rescue the hostages. Helicopters faced a storm in the desert and were damaged. One helicopter hit the airplane and caused a fire in it. European allies of the United States were astonished; they expressed their disagreement and considered it a military action against Iran. It is not finished yet, and is possible that it continues.

Banisadr attributed uneasiness in the universities to this event. Ayatollah Khomeini sent a very harsh message, and said, the "hostages are in danger. We will scatter them in different cities so that their rescue is not possible by military action." The situation has gotten more complicated, and there is no hope for any solution. The failure of the United States has overshadowed everything else.

MAY 1, 1980

A hostage-taking event happened in the Islamic Republic of Iran embassy in London. Five armed persons took twenty-three people hostage and demanded the release of ninety people in Khuzistan. Among the hostages were two reporters from the BBC and one English policeman. Once again, chaos has happened in Iran. Iranians say these people are Iraqi. English police say that they are Arabic-speaking Iranians. Police have rounded the embassy and given the hostage takers up to noon to release the prisoners; if so, they will be given an airplane to go away.

Now a new problem has occurred. Internal war is going on. The police, the Pasdaran, and the Kurds did not accept the ceasefire. Yesterday, two hundred were killed in Kurdistan and more than one thousand injured. The Kurds say they will continue fighting until they get autonomy.

People in the United States are angry about the film they saw on TV where Khalkhali made ugly gestures to murdered Americans. They justify an army attack on Iran. Cyrus Vans, the foreign affairs minister, resigned from his job in protest against the actions by U.S. troops.

MAY 7, 1980

Anti-terrorist group of England entered the embassy. Five terrorists and two of the hostages were killed, and the embassy was blown up. It was terrifying when people in England watched the direct report from TV and witnessed that terrorists killed one of the hostages, threw him out of the window, and announced that they will kill one person every half hour. Then the police went to the site and blew up the embassy from the air.

They captured one of the terrorists, killed the rest, and released twenty hostages. At this time, it seems that the event has ended. It is said that the action by the English Police will affect the American hostages. The English government is trying to stop the United States from carrying out a military attack in Iran.

The second phase of the election will be started in two days, while the failures of the first phase is not yet investigated and announced. The cabinet will be shuffled soon, and the ministers that are elected for Parliament will be discarded.

JUNE 2, 1980

The name of the Majlis Shouray Melli (the national parliament) has changed to the Islamic Parliament, and they are busy investigating the credibility of the representatives. They will start their work in a few days. Today an international conference was held in Tehran to investigate the American crimes in Iran. The U.S. government has foreseen hard punishments for those who attend this conference and will forbid their entry onto American soil.

In a TV interview, President Banisadr stated that he is critical about what happened so far; they were unsuccessful and could not return security to the country and improve the economical situation and provide job and shelter for people. He blamed the arbitrary decision making centers. Apparently, Dr. Habibi, his friend, will not be confirmed by Parliament for the prime minister's job. Instead, they have proposed Kalantry, the minister of roads, to be prime minister.

President Banisadr criticized the killings that were done by Khalkhali in the name of fighting against narcotics. Every day they kill a few people with this accusation.

Apparently, the government ruling prevailed in Kurdistan after heavy killings. It is said that the partisans escaped into the mountains and will continue their fighting.

No progress has been made in the matter of the American hostages. Ghotbzadeh said the investigation committee is not allowed to talk about the matter. Parliament is going to work on it. It is foreseen that their decision would be a trial of the hostages. The United States announced that a trial of the hostages will be deemed as an enemy action, and they will not tolerate it.

Economic sanctions did not work as expected; still an emergency budget and reduction of oil production to five hundred thousaned barrels a day is anticipated. The budget was planned for much more. They have in mind to reduce the salary of the government employees. While high prices still exist, this will cause even more dissatisfaction.

At last, the closing of the universities has been realized. They have taken examinations in a hasty manner. They will not open the universities until an Islamic program is prepared.

Every day there are rumors about a military attack on Iran. Many radio announcers speak about this matter and make it a hot topic. To obtain trusted news, people refer to foreign news agencies.

A committee for preventing forbidden things was held and is intervening in the private life of people and punishing them. They have in mind to make a design for the Islamic veil for women. This will cause dissatisfaction of many women, especially in Tehran.

MAY 14, 1980

The situation is dangerous; people expect something to happen. Days pass and wrongdoings and faults make the situation more complicated. President Banisadr clearly complains. Those in power do whatever they want to do. Due to the arrest of Khosrow Ghashghaee, the leader of Fars tribes and a Parliament representative, Shiraz and other cities in Fars are facing chaos. Yesterday a meeting with Mojahedin Khalgh was disturbed by Hezbollah. The Pasdaran's shooting resulted in twelve dead and three hundred injured, and caused shame of the authorities that were not able to control the case.

In Friday prayer, Moadikhah clearly attacked Banisadr and said that he should coordinate himself with Parliament. A difference in leadership surroundings became clear to the extent that Ayatollah Khomeini expressed his dissatisfaction. Authorities speak about the release of the hostages, but they do not know how to get rid of them.

Oil production was reduced to five hundred barrels a day. As a result, they are facing a shortage of budget and speak about reduction of employees' salaries. On groundless excuses, they expel employees.

The cutting of electricity and rationing of water consumption in the hot summer caused an inconvenience for people. In the middle of all of this, they have implemented a traffic plan and do not let private cars go inside the city, which causes delays in work and trouble for people. Domestic and foreign-made cigarettes are scarce, and the price is 200 to 250 rials a pack.

The high prices are terrible. We cannot hope for any progress as long as we have no security. An anti-revolution network was discovered in the army; they wanted to free Kurdistan. As the press, radio, and TV are under severe control, we do not hear anything from them.

Different stations have programs in Farsi during the day.

It is expected that the prime minister will introduce his cabinet to Parliament. It seems that it will be very difficult to have full consensus. It is difficult for Banisadr, because if the prime minister is elected who is not in accord with him, he will lose the rest of his power.

JUNE 14, 1980

In one month, a coup d'état Nowjeh was discovered in the army. Some people were killed and six hundred were arrested. It is possible that they were all executed. It is said that the coup d'état was organized by the United States, Israel, Iraq, and officers in the army and air force for return of Shapour Bakhtiar to power, which was discovered by Sepah Pasdaran. Banisadr said this was the sixth coup d'état that was found in four months. Another one was underway as well.

We are on the verge of falling down. Parliament approved credibility of their friends and with different excuses rejected the opposition. So far they did not start working, because they do not know the procedure in Parliament, and there are some other difficulties.

Banisadr was not able to introduce a prime minister to the Parliament. The Islamic Republic Party has many disputes. Some of the actions are disclosed through a video tape that was taken from the dialogue of Ayat, a Parliament representative, and was shown to people. Later they reconciled and forgot the matter. For some time, the subject of the Ayat tape became fun for people.

The Islamic veil became compulsory for women in public offices. Some women were resisting it, and they were immediately expelled; that became a lesson for others.

During Ramadan (a fasting month), there is pressure for acting on Islamic measures. At noon, every business is closed, and people go for prayer to the mosques. Women do not dare to appear in the streets without a veil. The sale of music records and tapes are forbidden. The courts for fighting narcotics and other Revolutionary Courts execute an average of ten people a day.

Recently, a new method of punishment started in Kerman, which is stoning. This surprised the world. Purification (Paksazi) committees at the government offices are working constantly and without mercy. They cut retirement for those who have cooperated with the ex-regime. Among them are old people who are not able to start another job. Private business is down, and few people may work for a living.

Last week, one American hostage was released due to sickness. Everybody is tired with the hostage taking, which resulted in economic sanction. They hope for a solution to end the crisis.

JUNE 19, 1980

Following the discovery of the coup d'état for the return of Shapur Bakhtiar, three hundred individuals were arrested, many from the army and air force.

Ayatollah Khomeini said, "Minor punishment for these people is death." So far, five people were executed, and it is foreseen that the rest will be executed soon.

Two days ago in Paris, a group that named themselves Pasdaran Islam attempted to kill Shapour Bakhtiar, the last prime minister in the Shah's regime. Bakhtiar escaped, but two policemen, one of them French, were killed. The terrorists were Palestinian with Syrian passports. They were captured by French police and are under investigation. The Islamic government denied any attachment to the plot. Sepah Pasdaran said that they condemn Bakhtiar to the death penalty.

Today the Islamic Parliament officially started their work and elected the board of directors and the Guardians Council. Hashemi Rafsanjani, founder of the Islamic Revolutionary Party, was elected as chairman. From now on, the country will be run by this party, whose leader is Ayatollah Beheshti. After finding out about the coup d'état, they said the National Front was helping them. With this excuse, Sepah Pasdaran occupied the party's office and forbid the demonstration they organized for the anniversary of 30 Tir for Dr. Mosaddegh and the toppling of Ghavamolsaltaneh's government.

Ahmad Madani, MP, from Kerman resigned from his job and did not appear before the Investigation Committee to answer their questions. He said this Parliament was not fit for him. The credibility of Khosrow Ghashghee was rejected for having cooperated with the Shah's regime. For this reason, a crisis has happened among the Fars tribes.

Two days ago in Oroumieh and Baluchestan, some Pasdars were killed. A public mourning was held for them.

Iran–Iraq borders are agitated by verbal fights. A recent relationship between Iran and Pakistan has become unfriendly.

The president of the Central Bank has expressed a dangerous economic situation and explained that inflation is 50 percent. Due to telling the truth, he has been summoned to the Revolutionary Court. He also protested against unrealistic layouts in the Central Bank and said he will personally investigate the files.

JULY 28, 1980

On July 27, the Shah passed away in Cairo. He fought cancer for seven years. The date of his death was the same that his father died sadly in a strange country thirty-six years ago. History will make its judgment about the Shah. Two years ago when he left the country, people celebrated and congratulated each other and offered candy while dancing in streets. Yesterday, people were indifferent. A few cars put their lights on. *Etellat* newspaper wrote "Shah Died," printed a terrible picture of him in his last days, and commented that CIA killed him.

Foreign news agencies spoke in detail and counted the positive and negative aspects of the Shah's era. In Egypt, one week of national mourning was announced. Anvarsadat, Egypt's president said that he will honor the Shah as the head of a country.

The Islamic republic announced the Shah's death with ugly words and insults. Surely a new era has started in the country which will be judged by history.

After some debate, the prime minister was elected. As was anticipated, it was Mirsalim, the chief of police and deputy minister of the Ministry of the Interior, and also a member of the Islamic Republic Party. Surely the ministers will be from the same suit.

The president said that in case the ministers are not acceptable to him, he will not take responsibility for them. What kind of government is this that the president and the cabinet have no understanding?

In a radio interview, Ghotbzadeh attacked the Islamic

Republic Party and the Student Followers of Imam's Line. Parliament summoned him for explanation. He will possibly not be in the future cabinet. The dispute was about the killing of Shapour Bakhtiar; he claimed the French police were aware of it, and information was given by Palestinians.

Student Followers of Imam's Line say that it was for the interest of the country. So far, the hot topic of the news agencies is about the coup d'état for which every day some people are going on trial and being condemned to death.

The Islamic Parliament is involved with internal disputes with no hope of solution. The situation is so complicated that even Dr. Ebrahim Yazdi wanted to resign, but Ayatollah Khomeini did not accept and said that they should not evacuate their positions.

AUGUST 4, 1980

A new chapter has started in the relationship between Iran and the United States. Two hundred students that were demonstrating against the Islamic Republic of Iran were arrested by the police and sent to prison with harsh contacts. The students did not mention their names to the police and went on a hunger strike that lasted for seven days. Students were confined in solitary cells in a New York prison and were at the mercy of Immigration Office investigators. It is possible that some of them will be deported. The case caused some protests inside and outside of Iran and became the topic of the day.

President Carter ordered the deportation of all students. Some negotiations may be going on for the release of the hostages in order for a release of the students. It is not yet confirmed. Apparently, the U.S. government authorized the students to make demonstrations. Some students demonstrated in front of the White House to sympathize with arrested students that faced cruel contacts. In some cases, they tried to feed them by force. So far, some of them have lost consciousness due to hunger. If something happens to a student - that makes the case more difficult.

Banisadr's situation is uncertain and shaky. He is not able to choose a prime minister. Beheshti, the chair of the Supreme Court, said that if Banisadr does not choose a prime minister, he will act on his authority and dismiss him. It is possible that such a decision is made; in that case, everything will be at the hands of the Islamic Republic Party that does not tolerate any other party. Pressure on the press has accelerated. At the moment, only the Islamic Republic Newspaper is circulating, but it has no buyers.

In Kurdistan, a big fight is going on between the Kurds and Sepah Pasdaran. It is said that one hundred people from the Pasdaran and army were killed.

Everyday some people are killed because of an accusation of narcotics or cooperation with the coup d'état. The Shariat Judge is the only person that is standing firm and works seriously; he makes personal decisions and does not listen to anyone and only kills, this person is Khalkhali – he who enjoys killing.

In Kerman, another person was stoned for unchaste actions. Such killings have not happened in hundred of years. Some prejudiced Islamic people, including the Islamic Republic Broadcast, confirmed it.

AUGUST 18, 1980

A wave of demonstration is taking place by members of the Islamic Students Association. They face harsh encounters everywhere. They do not give their names to the police and refrain from cooperation. Some are detained in London, which caused closure of the English embassy in Tehran.

Mohammad Ali Rejaee, the former minister of education, was elected as prime minister. He obtained a vote of confidence by Parliament, and the president accepted him. So far he did not introduce his cabinet. Hashemi Rafsanjani, the Parliament chairman, agreed with him. He wants the cabinet to be made entirely from the Islamic Republic Party.

The president escaped from an air accident. It is said that it was an assassination plot.

Rumors are spread that it was a military intervention to help President Carter win votes for his presidency. It is said that negotiations are going on for release of the hostages. The Iranian Parliament has maintained its position on no conciliation.

Ahmad Madani was accused of many crimes and is under persecution. He lost his position in Parliament and was summoned to the court.

Fighting between Iran and Iraq has become serious. The Abadan Refinery was hit by bombs and stopped working. The news made people worry and they rushed to gas stations and disturbed the city discipline. Radio and TV regularly ask people not to rush to gas stations. Traffic is slow, because most cars have no gas.

Iraq bombarded all the airports, and as a result, foreign flights are stopped. Iran has also bombarded Iraq stations and a refinery. The parties received very heavy damages from finance and human views.

Russia is helping Iraq with arms. The United States declared that it will not interfere in the war. So far, no government is seriously attempting to end this war.

It is planned that the schools will open today.

Apparently some problems happened and they changed the plan to a demonstration by teachers and students.

It seems that in the west of Iran, peace will never happen. Iraq's army first attacked Iran from western borders. They say they want back the lands they lost in the Algerian Treaty. Iraq closed the entry of the Shatolarab River, and they do not let the passage of vessels that do not carry the flag of Iraq. Now Iran is involved in internal and external wars.

The situation is terrible. Last night, all parts of Iran were in dark. People were recommended to go to their homes and have their radio and TV to listen to the messages. Ayatollah Khomeini said he will declare a jihad if necessary. Damage to the air force, marines, and infantry is heavy, and the same with Iraq. Foreign news agencies say that Iran's navy is better than Iraq's, but they have no solidarity and are not able to defend the country.

Iran has lost connection with the world. The only venue is radio.

The secretary general of the United Nations recommended the parties to settle their disputes by negotiation and avoid war. Yasser Arafat would like to mediate, but he has friendly relations with the two parties equally and cannot solve the problem.

In Iran, reserved army draftees are called to service; those who do not introduce themselves will be heavily punished. By order of Ayatollah Khomeini, the military courts stopped their work and gave the military staff a good raise. The elimination of generals in the army resulted in not having a good army to defend the country.

AUGUST 24, 1980

War between Iran and Iraq has become so dangerous and serious. Iraq has demolished the Abadan Refinery and Khark Island and is progressing toward Khoramshahr and Abadan. They occupied Mehran and Ghasreshin and penetrated inside Iranian territories.

Iranians bombarded a petrochemical factory, some refineries, and residential areas in Karkouk. The war between two oil-producer countries worries the Western countries and oil consumers. So far the proposals for mediation and negotiation did not work, and the two countries continue fighting in a stubborn way.

Living in Tehran has become so hard and unbearable. At night there is absolute darkness and danger of air attack. At night, going out is forbidden. The radio broadcasts military marches and notices.

So far, Tehran was attacked three times and the airport is closed. The Tehran Refinery was also attacked. The shortage of oil has made people uneasy.

As Iranian artilleries are mostly made in the United States, not having spare parts causes difficulty for the army. The United States stated that now Iran realized that they need peace. Most Arab countries supported Iraq. The Untied States asked Russia not to interfere with the war between Iran and Iraq, but in reality, the two super powers do so.

The United States said that when passage of ships that carry oil are stopped at Hormoz Strait, they have to make a military attack. Today a conference will be held between U.S.-friendly countries to find a solution for keeping the Hormoz Strait open. Iran is left alone.

The conditions of Iraq for accepting ceasefire are: self autonomy of Khuzestan, taking Great and Small Tombs and Abumousa, occupation of lands taken so far, and full authority on Shatolarab. None of these conditions are acceptable by Iran.

JULY 29, 1980

Tehran is passing stressful days and nights and is fighting at all boarders. The outside world does not know what is going on in Iran. They reflect whatever Iraq radio says. At present, the sensitive point of war is in Khuzestan.

Travelling inside the city is only possible by bus or taxi. Iran has not accepted negotiation and mediation from any country. Ziaolhagh, Pakistan's president and chairman of the Islamic Conference, and Habib Shati on behalf of Islamic government came to Tehran and returned without any solution. Conditions in Iraq are heavy. Today they added another condition that is autonomy of minorities, which means a full breakdown of the country and losing three islands and some lands on the western border.

JULY 31, 1980

After many nights of darkness, last night was almost quiet. In the streets, there was absolute darkness. People covered their windows with blankets to prevent the penetration of light.

Due to war and the explosion of the refineries, Iran is experiencing a shortage of oil. For a country that was one of the greatest oil exporters, buying oil from other countries is hard. It is not clear what will be the situation of oil export.

AUGUST 5, 1980

Last week the war between Iran and Iraq continued. Iran was able to make great damages to Iraq. Iraq was still not able to evacuate the Iraqis from Khuzestan. Iraqis suffered heavy damages for occupation of Dezful, Ahvaz, and Khoramshahr. Now Jordan is officially supporting Iraq and dispatched five thousand soldiers there and promised to do anything to help. Saudi Arabia, Egypt, and Kuwait are clearly supporting Iraq. The United States sold four AVAX developed airplanes to Saudi Arabia. It is not clear what will happen if Iraq uses the support facilities offered to them by allies. Airplanes used in fighting against Iran are made in Russia, the Mig and Topoloph planes. In the meeting of the Russian ambassador with the prime minister, they proposed selling arms to Iran as well.

Iran bombarded an atomic station in Iraq, which was built with the cooperation of France, and made minor damages. Israel used the case in their favor, and in opposition radio, it was said that the plan of this attack was given to Iran by Israel. Iraq declared a four-day ceasefire. In the case that it is broken by Iran, they will continue their attacks. In the first day of the ceasefire, the attacks were harder.

Yesterday the alarms sounded four times. The common army staff said in a bombardment near Tehran, two were killed and eight wounded. Air attacks in Tehran worried people. The Tabriz Refinery was hit by a rocket. The aim was the refinery. They once attacked Isfahan Refinery. Iranians destroyed oil stations and oil pipes in Iraq. In the Persian Gulf, many battleships of different countries are ready in case the Hormoz Strait is closed.

OCTOBER 7, 1980

Attacks by Iraq's airplanes continue. Yesterday they bombarded the Helicopter Factory, Iran National, residences in Ekbatan, and a few factories near Karaj. The operation started in the early afternoon and lasted until 6:00 AM. Iraqi airplanes dropped the bombs without having certain aim. Mehrabad Airport was attacked several times.

The president said that if we were fighting only with Iraq, we would be able to defeat them, but Iraq has friends, including Jordan and Egypt. The BBC announced that Khoramshahr is occupied by Iraq. Immediately, Khalkhali was interviewed from Khoramshahr and said that is not true.

Alarms, attacks, and bombardments confuse the news reporters. Yesterday, after an air attack by Iraq, alarms started to sound. Nights are stressful, mainly because people are not aware of what is going on. To give news to the press and radios is forbidden. Only the army commander staff is allowed to tell people what has happened.

Due to the shortage of oil, much work is being stopped and visiting friends is impossible. People who lost their jobs found a new job that is lined up out of necessity. There is no money left for the government to buy oil from other countries.

OCTOBER 12, 1980

After bombing Dezful and Andimeshk with ground-to-ground missiles and making heavy damages to people and garrisons, Tehran has been quiet for two days.

The United States asked Jordan not to interfere with the war between Iran and Iraq. Syria, who shows friendship with Iran, has signed a twenty-year treaty with Russia. It worries other governments to see the Middle East having tendencies toward Marxism. Iran is trying to have a better relationship with Russia. Russia has denied the proposal by Prime Minister Rajai for the sale of artilleries. They did not expect their secret negotiations to be disclosed.

Ayatollah Khomeini has delegated the authorities on war and the related matters to the High Council of Defense, and he allowed Hashemi Rafsanjani from Parliament to participate in negotiations. This happened after criticism of Banisadr from Khomeini. It is possible that the clerics are worried about unity between the army and Banisadr.

From a foreign policy viewpoint, the government decided to take part in a general meeting of the United Nations. In the first day, some disputes happened between Iran and Iraq representatives.

The United States is severely protecting the Oil Resources of Saudi Arabia and other countries in the Persian Gulf to compensate for the shortage of oil in Iran and Iraq, around eighteen million barrels a day. The Persian Gulf is full of vessels from different countries to prevent the closure of the Hormoz Strait. Iran will not make any trouble for vessels that carry the UN flag, provided that Iraq accepts the same conditions.

The war between Iran and Iraq has reached a dead end. Both parties lost their artilleries and human resources. People in Khuzestan are defending their cities without any consideration of the difference in beliefs, and they put pressure on Iraq. Iraq made a bridge over the Karun River for sending artilleries and personnel.

At the western border, it is fight and flight. The general assembly of the United Nations and the Security Council are ready to investigate the differences between the two countries.

Iran will accept if it is in their favor.

OCTOBER 18, 1980

War continues vigorously. Iraq claims that it has tightened blockage of Abadan and Khoramshahr and bombarded Tabriz and Kermanshah. Prime Minister Rajai went to New York to take part in a meeting of the Security Council and said he will only negotiate about war between Iran and Iraq. President Carter announced that he will support and respect the independence of Iran and blames Iraq, who has penetrated Iranian territories. He said they are ready to sell arms to Iran if they accept it. Iran stands firm and says that it is ready to accept the decision of the United Nations when it condemns Iraq and expels Iraqi troops from Iranian lands.

Iraq complained that Iran interfered in Iraq. This stupid war is a big loss to the parties, and they will not be able to recover for many years.

Foreign radios say some negotiations for release of the hostages are on the way. For the Islamic republic, it is a shame to cooperate with the United States, but it is also a shame if they do not receive some help. They will have a harder time with Iraq that is supported by Arab countries. The political situation is very difficult.

Iraq expressed readiness for a ceasefire. Iran said that it will not agree with ceasefire as long as Iraq is in Iranian lands. Iran let the vessels with UN flags pass Shatolarab, but Iraq did not agree with it.

Iraq is attacking residential areas, hospitals, and schools, causing heavy damages. To supply oil to the provinces has become a difficult task, because all refineries are out of service. Oil is given in rations: gas is thirty liters a month, and oil is twenty liters a week. The oil portion is not enough for consumption during winter time. Those who can afford it buy oil from the black market. Bigger portions of oil are assigned to physicians.

To purchase arms and oil, Iran sold some gold reserves in international markets. Western countries have enough oil reserves for the time being.

OCTOBER 26, 1980

Prime Minister Rajai took part in the Security Council. He criticized the United States and played the role of victim, which did not affect anyone. These were not new statements. So far the decision of the Security Council is not issued. Rajai said whatever their decision is we will do our own job, which means expel Iraq from Iranian lands.

In addition to Abadan and Khoramshahr, where war is house to house, Dezful and Ahvaz are under the blockage of Iraqi soldiers and missile attacks. Iraq exploded the great pipeline that carries oil to Tehran.

In the United States, as the presidential election draws near, hope for freedom of the hostages is used as propaganda for more votes. If the hostages are not released in one week's time, it would not be good for the election of President Carter. If Carter is not re-elected, Iran has to deal with Reagan, who said he would not bear this shame for the United States.

America announced that they will free Iranian deposits of eight billion dollars and remove the sanction, which means sell spare parts for artilleries and make the relationship between the two countries normal. The Islamic Republic of Iran is in a position that may accept the conditions to avoid division of the territory, and it is seeking support for the Iranian army.

Iraq stated that if the delivery of spare parts to Iran happens, it means that the United States is not neutral in the war between Iran and Iraq, and a third world war is inevitable. Iran will now buy arms from Russia.

It was decided that Islamic Parliament will provide conditions for the release of the hostages. The United States hopes that Iranian conditions are suitable and they can accept them. The conditions possibly would be: release of Iranian deposits, removal of an economic sanction, and no interference in Iran. It seems the conditions are acceptable to the United States. It is said that the U.S. companies that had investments in Iran will receive compensation from Iranian deposits. U.S. Courts have already confirmed the case. Very crucial days are passing in Iran and in the United States. If Iran does not make the deal, the United States will be ready for a real war.

OCTOBER 27, 1980

Khoramshahr is occupied by Iraq, and its connection with other cities is cut. Due to plenty of bloodshed, they call this city "Khounin Shahr," meaning bloody city. Iraqis call it "Mohamereh," the old name of the city. The surrounding of Ababdan is tight. If the same keeps going on, Khuzestan would be in danger of separation from Iran.

Foreign radios speak about the near release of the hostages. They even provided a hospital, airplane, photographer, and journalist. It is said that the Algerian government has interfered in the matter.

Iranians are in constant worry. They are sad about the war, refuge of Iranians, murder of many, and losing some of their lands. Nights are most breathtaking. Darkness and winter has depressed us all. During the long hours of night, the only hobby is listening to the radio in order to connect us with other parts of the world. Overseas radio broadcasts the Iran–Iraq war frequently. Local radio is either assaults or telling lies. People hate Islamic radio and TV and do not listen or watch them. We may hear Iranian poetry and music from foreign radios.

When we are freezing from cold, we do not start a heater; we think of the time that has been wasted to get that much oil. Our foods are almost half-cooked. We try to use very little gas, because we do not know what will happen tomorrow.

They accuse people of being anti-revolution and detain them. People do not like to get together; they are afraid of being accused of some sort of crime, such as being a spy, and losing their heads.

Slogans of the Islamic republic in the beginning were "Freedom, Independence, Islamic Republic." What remains from those slogans is only "Islamic Republic," against losing parts of the territory and life of many people.

OCTOBER 30, 1980

Exactly two days before the election in the United States, Islamic Parliament announced the conditions for release of American hostages, assuming that will help the election of President Carter. Conditions were: no interfere of the United States in Iranian affairs; return of the Shah's assets; release of Iranian deposits; and, refraining from any claim against the hostage taking. Each of these conditions requires very complicated financial and political procedures. Iran's announcement did not help President Carter in his election, and he failed the election to Reagan. Although Reagan said he will not be in charge before January 20, 1981, Carter has to consult with him. Reagan's friends, Kissinger,

Rockefeller, and Ford, are all the Shah's friends and oppose the Islamic Republic of Iran.

One week has already passed, and the United States has not responded to the proposals of the Islamic Republic of Iran. Some of them are out of the president's capacity. The new government of the United States will not sell arms to Iran, but it is possible to give them the spare parts that were paid for during the Shah's time. The world is worried that if the United States gives Iran spare parts, Russia will do the same and give Iraq artilleries, and thus start the third world war.

War is expanding. After Algeria, no attempts have been made for mediation.

Some of the regime spies said that the army is not fighting seriously. Ayatollah Montazeri criticized them and said it is better that Ayatollah Khomeini be the commander in chief. Disagreement among groups is quite clear. The president and the Islamic republic that have access to all public resources do not agree with each other.

In a TV interview, Ghotbzadeh, the ex-director of Radio and TV and the previous minister of foreign affairs, along with a clergy friend of the president made harsh criticisms of the Islamic Republic Party and disclosed some of their secrets. Immediately, they faced a reaction that was the dismissal of the clergy and arrest of Ghotbzadeh, who was sent to Evin Prison. This hasty action made people aware that this government does not tolerate any critique, even from those who played major roles in the victory of the Islamic republic. The arrest of Ghotbzadeh was broadcasted by foreign media.

Recently it was announced that, in addition to gas and oil, meat, chicken, eggs, washing powder, cigarettes, and cooking oil will be rationed. All this will be under supervision of clergies and mosques, which are supposed to be for prayer but will be transformed to a supermarket in order to give all people equal portions. None of the promises are realized. It was arranged that every family receives twenty liters of oil a week; now they give thirty liters a month, which is not enough for cooking and heating. Electricity is also portioned, and it is not possible to use an electric heater.

NOVEMBER 15, 1980

Conditions put forward by Iran were not acceptable to the United States. Varen Christofer, the deputy minister of U.S. foreign affairs, handed the disapproval to Iranian authorities in Algeria. Iran and the United States did not show any reaction. The United States kept their response secret.

The secretary general of the United Nations appointed Olof Palme, the ex-prime minister of Sweden, to investigate the views of Iran and Iraq and find a solution for a ceasefire. Olof Palme has a history of mediation in Iranian disputes and will soon go to Iran and then Baghdad. He confessed that this is a very difficult task.

Yesterday, Iraq made hard attacks on Iranian territory. The result was the fall of four airplanes, four tanks, and some people.

NOVEMBER 26, 1980

The U.N. assignee returned to New York and expressed his disappointment. President Banisadr said that with the heavy damages to the Iraq army, we are close to the end of war. When he returned from Khuzestan, President Banisadr complained to people about the bad management of the government. Authorities in the

Islamic Republic Party that saw themselves attributed to those remarks responded to the allegations. Ayatollah Khomeini ordered the two parties to stop the disputes and be silent.

Last week, a few masked persons attacked *Mizan* newspaper and looted their office, which caused a lot of protests. The newspaper will be published, but the publishers feel very threatened and will censor themselves. The Islamic revolution newspaper, which is published by the president, sometimes cautiously publishes news.

Ayatollah Khomeini warned the newspapers to be aloof; otherwise, he will punish them. Nobody is allowed to speak about the disputes among the authorities. Hashemi Rafsanjani, the chairman of Parliament, made a trip to Libya, Algeria, and Lebanon to explain the policy of Iran and he will travel more in this regard.

Kissinger, Reagan's advisor, said that if the hostages are not released by January 20, Iran will be responsible for the consequences. The Iranian president said he did not interfere with the hostage affairs and was opposed from the beginning.

To find shelter for the war homeless has become a very acute problem. They try to settle them in different provinces so that Tehran is not crowded. Most of these homeless go to Tehran to seek a place to live in.

The losses from the war are so great that even if war is over, we cannot recover easily. In Iraq, people over sixty-five and farmers are called for service. The Arab countries wanted to start a conference, even though Libya, Algeria, and the Palestine Freedom Front disagreed. It is possible that Iraq can attract their support. Iran is isolated in this war and needs Western countries to provide spare parts for the artilleries. Due to sanction, the delivery of spare parts is impossible.

DECEMBER 9, 1980

Nowadays, governments are busy with the crisis in Poland. Any day, Russia and its allies may make a military attack on Poland, which is fighting to gain freedom from communism. In such a case, the United States and its allies will not be neutral.

The Iran–Iraq War has lost face. Iraq started to export oil through Syria, who pretended to be a friend of Iran. But in Iran, the oil situation gets worse every day. Internal disputes are accelerated. The president has a disagreement with the clergies. The clergies make people demonstrate against the president. U.S. radio disclosed that Banisadr asked Ayatollah Khomeini to make Rajai, the prime minister, resign from his job due to his incapability. He also said he was ready to resign his job, but it is not to the interest of the country and will cause the failure of Iran in front of Iraq. The army is supporting the president; Sepah Pasdaran supports the clergies. Their disagreement is drawn to the schools; fighting between students of high schools has resulted in the injury of students.

DECEMBER 20, 1980

A letter from the president to Ayatollah Khomeini has circulated in which he criticizes Rajai and says he is incapable of solving the problems of the country. In the letter, he said that if we do not free the American hostages in good will, we have to do it in a weak position, which has already happened. He wished himself dead to make himself free from the trouble and wished not to see the defeat of Iran. Some MP supporters of the Islamic Republic Party asked the president to be persecuted, because he revealed the negotiations of a closed meeting of Parliament to the Islamic revolution newspaper. Fighting between the two internal wings goes on.

Clergies headed by Ayatollah Montazeri asked people to make a demonstration in support of the clergies on Thursday, December 18, which was prohibited by Ayatollah Khomeini. In cities, pictures of Ayatollah Montazeri were torn out and some slogans were chanted about the clergies.

The media was informed that in Rezaeeyeh a confrontation happened between people in which one hundred anti-revolutionaries, twelve army men, and the Pasdaran's staff were killed.

Iraq said that the fighting will continue until springtime. Every day millions of dollars worth of arms vanish and many people are killed.

The number of homeless persons is more than one million and has made for an acute problem for the government. They are people who had some sort of job and a home. Now they are war stricken and need to be supported by the government. Further natural disaster makes trouble as well. Last night, an earthquake of 5.7 on the Richter scale trembled Tehran and the central region of Iran. It resulted in twenty-five dead and a great number injured. Damages are many. The golden minaret of Imamzadeh Masoum is cracked.

The government declared that it has accepted the claims of American companies carrying Iranian deposits to Algerian banks and guaranteeing the assets of the Shah. It seems that Americans are not in a hurry and said that they should not expect the hostages' freedom before Christmas.

Some people are trying to open universities, but Ayatollah Khomeini told them he will not let them open until they are fully Islamic.

JANUARY 22, 1981

At last the fifty-two American hostages were released, which was exactly twenty-five minutes after the end of Carter's presidency. The two countries tried to do it before Reagan came to power and not give him an excuse for attacking Iran. The process of releasing the Iranian deposits was very complicated and took about ten days' time of the European and American banking systems. The transfer of Iran's assets from the United States to the Central Bank of England was the greatest banking transaction in the world. After calculations, from eight billion deposits, only 2.8 billion dollars cash was transferred to Algeria to be available to the Iranian government when the hostages are free. Iranian debts were deducted, and some money was held for the possible claims of American companies against Iran, which has to be referred to international arbitration.

There is no mention of the return of the Shah and his family's assets. A government speaker said they had enough time to take their assets out of the country.

After 444 days of detention, the hostages were freed under the supervision of the Student Followers of Imam's Line. Great celebrations were held in the United States. Hostages were taken to an army hospital to be checked and to see whether they have the possibility of starting a normal life or not.

The release of the hostages was considered a great victory for Iran; the same as taking them. They declared that whoever thinks otherwise is anti-revolution.

Media in the United States started to disclose the

torture of the hostages. To avoid any problem so far, they refrained from disclosing the secrets. The sanction against Iran ended. Foreign trade may possibly be normalized.

JANUARY 26, 1981

It is said that the president and the people of Iran were cheated, and the conditions set by Parliament are not being observed.

Iran refrained from taking part in the conference for presidents of Islamic governments because Saddam Hussein was there, and they would discuss the matter of returning the three islands (two Tombs and Abumousa) to the United Arab Emirates.

Although the sanction was removed by the United States - European countries and Japan are still not ready to sell arms to Iran. The fight between Iran and Iraq is going on, and there is no news about mediation by Olof Palme, the representative of the United Nations.

Disagreement among government authorities is continuing. Banisadr started to make speeches that were welcomed by the people.

The United States spoke with coarse language about Iran. Reagan called Iran a terrorist government and said, "Iran is a lawless land." Iranian newspapers started to make the same gestures.

FEBRUARY 4, 1981

The political atmosphere in Iran is unstable. War is more serious in Kurdistan. Ayatollah Khomeini gave them until February 11, the anniversary of the revolution, to surrender or face the consequences.

France sold thirty-five Mirage airplanes to Iraq, and West Germany announced that it will sell arms to Saudi

Arabia. The delivery of four AVAX by the United States to Saudi Arabia are signs of acceleration of war.

Aghashahi, the foreign affairs minister of Pakistan, is coming to Tehran and will visit the president and the prime minister to find a solution to end the fight. Banisadr is fighting with the clergies on different fronts. Recently, he said that people should confront club holders the same as they did in Isfahan. So disagreement between the groups is getting more acute.

It is decided that Banisadr will make a speech in Azadi Square on February 11, the anniversary of the revolution. For exactly the same day, the Islamic Republic Party has announced a demonstration. There is a possibility of direct attack by the United States on Iran. Reagan said, "Carter should not negotiate and make agreement with the Iranian government and must use force from the very beginning."

France stated that if Iran wants to receive the small battleships that are paid for, they should pay the claims of French companies, which is about one billion dollars. The United States deems it possible to deliver spare parts through European countries. In such case, they will also ask for their claims.

England managed to sign two contracts for purchase of oil. Iran exports about six hundred thousand barrels of oil a day and is looking for buyers.

High prices are keeping people under pressure. If the authorities can find a solution to their disagreements, the situation will get better.

Rajai is not popular and some protests are made against him in Parliament.

FEBRUARY 26, 1981

At last part of the Iranian deposits were freed. The

internal situation is as bad as it was, and people are under pressure for the shortage of oil in wintertime.

Today it was decided that three MPs, Bazargan, Sahabi, and Sabaghian, will speak in a big gathering in Amjadieh, especially on the phenomenon of club fighting that is used to oppress the opposition.

Lahooti, an MP from Rasht and a friend of Ayatollah Khomeini, escaped from an assassination attempt. Recently he criticized the regime. Ahmad Khomeini (Ayatollah Khomeini's son) issued a notice to the government and Parliament in regard to preventing an attack on demonstrations.

Chaos in the universities has spread to the high schools. The Kharazmi girls and boys high schools are closed. It is possible the other schools are also closed. To avoid protests, the government decided to close offices for one week and the schools for two weeks. The bus union protested their new year bonus and started a strike. The government very quickly responded and announced that those who go on strike will be referred to the Revolutionary Court and treated with the rules of war time.

Olof Palme, the representative of the United Nations that failed in his first assignment, will come back to Iran with eight other people and try to solve the disputes between Iran and Iraq.

The disagreement between Banisadr and Rajai continues. In a TV interview, Rajai said, "I am afraid that the Islamic revolution is transformed to execution revolution."

The government has submitted a bill to Parliament with regard to purification and renovation of human resources. Some representatives asked its withdrawal. Another bill that was submitted to Parliament is called

Ghesas, which means revenge. Its rules are taken from the Koran, such as killing, separating limbs, blinding, and other savage rules that give a terrible picture of the Islamic society. Lawyers protested these bills. With the majority of the Islamic Republic Party in Parliament, there is a possibility of the approval of these bills.

MARCH 7, 1981

A delegation from the Islamic Conference came to Iran to solve the problems between Iran and Iraq and submitted a plan for a ceasefire that was not acceptable by Iran. This high-ranking delegation consisted of four presidents, Turkey's prime minister, and the secretary general of the Islamic conference. They negotiated two times with Ayatollah Khomeini and prayed at his back.

Iran explained its position as follows: a ceasefire and departure of Iraqi soldiers should be simultaneous, and the Algeria Treaty needs to be recognized as valid and the aggressor identified and punished.

In the president's speech on the anniversary of Dr. Mosaddegh, great chaos happened, and it resulted in an issue of a new order and made more trouble. In the speech, some people chanted slogans against the president. He asked people to catch the attackers and deliver them to police. While catching these people, some knives and hand weapons were found, and the president showed the identity cards to the audience. During Friday prayer, these actions were condemned and many slogans against the president were chanted. Banisadr requested a trial of those people, and asked people to testify what they saw. Now fighting has prevailed, and the two parties accuse each other. In the meantime, Ayatollah Khomeini said he will not receive any visitor for one week. Either club fighting is stopped or no more gatherings will happen.

APRIL 9, 1981

Contrary to insisting on no celebration of Chahar-Shanbeh Suri (the last Wednesday of the year) and Norooz (the Iranian New Year), two national days, they were remembered very well. When a country is in war, it should honor and respect its nationality more than usual and use it to stand in front of the enemy.

On April 1, it was arranged to have a great demonstration for the anniversary of the Islamic republic, but it was cancelled due to rain and snow falling.

Efforts to end the war are continuing, but so far it does not work.

Iranian pilots have bombed the Iraq stations from inside that country and caused great damages. They have taken air photographs from Iraq's Parliament and stated that they did not intend to hit the residential areas.

Mizan newspaper, which was placed under a ban, started with help given by Bazargan and members of the temporary cabinet. This time Reza Sadr, the director in charge, was arrested and the newspaper went under ban again. Public prosecutors stop every newspaper that publishes critical articles; they also forbid any demonstrations and strikes. Prosecutors asked the armed groups to deliver their arms to Sepah Pasdaran.

The three-person committee that was assigned to solve the disputes between Banisadr and the government has started its work. Ayatollah Khomeini banned any speech that causes disagreement among the groups.

Newspapers are forbidden to criticize. So, no opposing statement is heard.

JUNE 4, 1981

Nothing new has happened; everything goes on in the same routine, meaning war and disputes among authorities. The only happening was the interview of the president with the media on opposing Parliament, the cabinet, and the Islamic Republic Party. His last request was to ask the people's views in a referendum. That was hard for his opponents, and they attacked him harder. The three-person committee accused him of disobedience of Ayatollah Khomeini's orders, which means he should be persecuted. The cases of disobedience were: not signing the law which passed by Parliament and made the prime minister responsible for those ministries that had no minister; and the president did not report his assets to the High Judicial Council. Recently a bill has been passed by Parliament that limits the authority of the president and delegates them to the prime minister. Appointment of the head of the Central Bank and Red Cross were omitted from the authorities of the president. Noubary, the head of the Central Bank, opposed the Algeria Treaty and freedom of the hostages and said it was not in the interest of Iran. The authorities took aim at him and found a few cases of errors for him, and it is possible that he will be persecuted as well. Noubary is a close friend of the president, and Rajai said he has no understanding with him.

Banisadr is in a very unpleasant situation, but he is not giving up. It seems that with losing the power of decision making and the serious opposing by the government authorities, he has no choice but to give up. The reason that the opposition does not go further is that they are worried about justification of negative effects of omitting the president on the Iran–Iraq war. Banisadr spends almost all his time on the fronts and is popular among army staff.

While war still continues, Iran returns some of the lands that were occupied by Iraq. Mediation of different groups did not work so far. One of the problematic issues is budget and the export of oil. The budget is still not ratified to this date. They have approved one-third of the budget and approved an eight hundred billion rials expense from the government. Most of it has been spent on war expenses.

Recently a contract for one billion pounds was signed with the English company Talbut for making cars. It is now under investigation. It is not clear why they concluded such a contract for making a car that has no priority.

At last the trial of Amir Entezam, the minister without portfolio during the temporary cabinet, has started. Student Followers of Imam's Line disclosed that he had some sort of connection with the United States. Actually, all members of the temporary cabinet of Bazargan are accused of something. So far the final verdict is not issued. It was disclosed that before the revolution, the Islamic representatives were in touch with the United States.

With regard to accusations to the president, two of his advisors were arrested; one for seizing the documents of the Foreign Affairs Ministry, and the other for corruption and helping the Shah's friends send money abroad.

Other chaos included the beating of Salamatian, the president's friend in Parliament, by a Hamadan representative and threatening him by knife. He said that was because of his opposing the budget.

AUGUST 13, 1981

Ayatollah Khomeini dismissed Banisadr from the commander-in-chief position, which was followed by a wave of happiness in a demonstration. The radio changed its normal schedule to songs and slogans in favor of Ayatollah Khomeini. Anti-Banisadr ideas are getting so hot that some people around his office were asking for his execution. The president is deprived of all types of contact with the people. The Islamic republic newspaper is banned, and all demonstrations are forbidden. As a result, the president has no way to tell people what happened and is drawn to a dead end. Parliament will possibly do something about him and dismiss him from the presidency. Contrary to expectations of Banisadr, the army and people do not support him. The Public Prosecutor's Office has banned demonstrations; therefore, those who were supporting the president have no possibility of showing up.

Since newspapers with critical views are banned, and much propaganda against the president is on the radio and TV, some other incidents may happen. All government organizations are at the disposal of the majority party.

The position of the minorities in Parliament is miserable. If they say something, the others condemn them and make ugly remarks against them. They dare not to speak. Army Commanders supported Ayatollah Khomeini in an interview. It is said that the army had some success in the war against Iraq.

The hot topic is the bombardment of the Atomic Station of Iraq by Israel, which was highly criticized.

Israel claims that Iraq had plans to make atomic bombs, which endangered Israel.

A strong earthquake in Golbaf, a city in Kerman, leveled the city and killed all of the inhabitants. It was a great disaster for the Kerman people. Three thousand people were killed. Now they have to try to find the corpses.

In an interview with Reuters, Banisadr stated that, "a coup d'état is done against me, and I am in danger." After the interview, the Pasdaran surrounded the residence of the president and banned any contact with him.

JUNE 21, 1981

There was a big show in Parliament. Two-thirds of the MPs asked for dismissal of the president for his political incapability and made many accusations against him. Many Hezbollah members were ready around Parliament, and by order of the prosecutor general, asked for execution of the president. After dismissal from the commander-in-chief position, Banisadr did not appear in public. Ayatollah Khomeini asked him to repent for his behavior on TV. Banisadr did not do so and issued two short notices that showed he had not changed his mind.

Banisadr escaped from Iran. The presidents of France and Turkey said that if he applies refugee status, they will grant it to him. Some said he is hiding in Hamedan, his hometown.

Mojahedeen has proclaimed armed fighting against Iran to support Banisadr. Street fighting started in Tehran. So far thirty people are killed and some are wounded. The government stated that they will have a hard confrontation with Mojahedeen.

A demonstration by the National Front party was

anticipated for June 15, but before that date, the prosecutor general ordered Hezbollah to stop it. Ayatollah Khomeini asked the political groups to announce that they have no connection with the National Front. Bazargan expressed his loyalty to Ayatollah Khomeini through stating that Nehzat Moghavemat (the political party) received no order for participation in the demonstration. Still, an order by the prosecutor general for the arrest of him and his friends was issued.

Members of the president's office and his closest friends were all arrested. Today the final session of Parliament about the incapacity of the president was held. Parliament voted for his dismissal. It is possible that after dismissal, he will be called for trial. In Parliament, three MPs spoke in favor of the president. Minorities did not participate in the session due to not having security. Azam Taleghani, in favor of the president, stated "why Parliament voted for dismissal of the president. I shall follow the case up to toppling the Islamic Republic."

The government is concerned about demonstrations by the president's friends and the others who are displeased. It is a pity that in an Islamic regime the first president became so humiliated and witnessed the method of fighting with him.

One month ago, everybody was silent; after his dismissal from commander in chief, they started to attack him harshly. They do not mind executing him. Nobody mentioned his services and what he has done in the position of commander in chief. In this regime, everything is either black or white, nothing in between.

Mojahedin are sacrificing and will make an armed fight against the regime. It seems that difficult days are in front of us, and more people will be killed. At the present time, the hot topic is the dismissal of the president.

Olof Palme came to Iran once more to mediate the war between Iran and Iraq. Although his past efforts did not work, maybe now that the decision making centers are reduced, he could do something.

JUNE 28, 1981

From the date that Parliament voted for dismissal of the president, he has been hidden and searching for him did not work. There are rumors that he has gone to Kurdistan, out of Iran, or to Egypt.

Chamran, the representative of Ayatollah Khomeini in the High Council of Defense and a candidate for commander in chief, was killed in the war front. Chamran was a specialist in partisan wars and the founder of Sepah Pasdaran. He fought for many years in the south of Lebanon with the Shiites front and was a key personnel in the Islamic Republic of Iran.

After the disappearance of Banisadr, many of his followers were arrested and executed. Once more the wave of executions by the Revolutionary Court accelerated. Amnesty International asked the head of governments to request that Ayatollah Khomeini stop the executions. The Islamic republic does not like such interference and thinks of them as being fed by imperialism.

At Friday prayer, Imam Jome, Khamenee MP and Ayatollah Khomeini's representative in the High Council of Defense, escaped from an attempted killing. The attempt was made by a bomb in the speaker. He was wounded on his right chest and hand. He immediately had surgery, and one of his hands became numb.

Although he was bleeding heavily, the doctors declared that the danger was removed.

Mid-term elections of the provinces that were not performed because of opposition by the president have been done. To run the country, a Presidency Council was appointed that consists of the chair of Supreme Court, prime minster, and a chairman of Parliament. The date of election of a new president is in a month.

So far, only Rajai, the prime minister, is a candidate from the Islamic Republic Party. The minister of foreign affairs, who was not appointed by the ex-president, was immediately appointed.

When Mojahedin announced an armed fight, some of their leaders were executed. It was announced that four hundred of them will be executed soon. Worry about revenge from the two parties is evident.

JULY 2, 1981

At 9:30 AM on Thursday, June 7, a powerful bomb exploded in the salon of the Islamic Republic Party, where the leaders were gathered, and seventy-four of them were killed. Among them was Ayatollah Beheshti, the most powerful man after Ayatollah Khomeini, secretary general of the party, and member of the Presidency Council. He was the brain and planner of the Islamic Republic Party, with many enemies and opponents. Four ministers—the minister of power, the minister of labor, the minister without portfolio, and the minister of telecommunication—twenty MPs, and eight deputy ministers were among the group killed. A two-day public holiday and one week of mourning was announced. A very crowded burial ceremony was planned for them.

By killing twenty MPs, it is possible that Parliament

cannot continue its work. Some negotiations were carried on with the leader of the opposition group, Bazargan. They decided to attend Parliament sessions provided that they were given time for speaking and people stopped insulting them outside of Parliament. Some wounded MPs were brought to Parliament on their wheelchairs. Those elected two days back were brought to Parliament before their credibility was approved. Thus, it was announced that Parliament is in quorum.

Among the assassinated persons was Mohammad Montazery, the son of Ayatollah Montazeri, who organized a terrorist operation at Mehrabad Airport and was the main enemy of the temporary cabinet of Bazargan.

Mojahedeen Khalgh, who are not accepted by the authorities, declared that they had nothing to do with the explosion and did not accept the responsibility of the manslaughter. The government sees the United States, Nationalists, the left wing, Zionists, and in short every group responsible for the event. Replacement for killed ministers and the chief of the Supreme Court was done quickly. They tried to keep the situation in normal mode.

Hunting for the opposition, including Mojahedeen, started, and their execution is going on even with the protest of internal and external authorities. The public prosecutor announced that Evin Prison will be closed to visitors due to the many trials that are currently going on. Mojahedeen Khalgh declared that they will refrain from street demonstrations and instead will carry out bombing.

Dismissed President Banisadr issued a statement that said he is the president and not to value the vote of

Parliament. He asked to speak directly to the public to disclose secrets of the authorities. So far his hiding place has not been found.

Rajai, the prime minister, Behzad Nabavi, the government speaker, Bahonar, the minister of culture, and Rafsanjani, the chairperson of Parliament, were present in the meeting of the Islamic Republic Party and departed in time before the explosion. After the attempted killing of Khamenee, the Friday Imam, Rafsanjani was appointed to the job.

Nowadays, Tehran streets witness demonstrations of the Hezbollah Party that frighten people. The radio and TV are broadcasting slogans without any interruption. No newspaper is published, except by partisans of the Islamic republic.

Bahonar, the secretary general of the Islamic Republic Party, was appointed as the minister of culture and higher education.

JULY 7, 1981

Ten team houses of Mojahedeen Khalgh were discovered, and arms were confiscated and many of them arrested. Twenty-three in Tehran and four in the provinces were executed. Gilan, the governor general, was assassinated. The news regularly announces killings that are attributed to the United States and Mojahedeen Khalgh.

Ayatollah Khomeini religiously orders people to identify the opposition and deliver them to Sepah Pasdaran.

The nomination for presidency has started. Mehdi Bazargan, the first prime minister of the temporary government, Kianoori, the leader of the Toudeh Party, and Farokh Negahdar, the leader of Fadaeean Khalgh, are all friends of the Islamic republic and nominated themselves for presidency. Elections in the cities where their MPs were killed will be renewed.

Seventy-four people were killed; to commemorate martyrdoms in Karbala, they call them seventy-two martyrdoms. The bomber was found; it was the person in charge of the conference hall. He has gone undercover after the bombing.

Ayatollah Khomeini announced that he will not visit anybody during the fasting month of Ramadan. In every ministry and organization, they have installed powerful speakers to air prayers and the Koran.

The arrest and execution of Mojahedin Khalgh, who are called Monafeghin (betrayers), are continuing. Their activities in the publication of newsletters and demonstrations are absolutely banned. Minority groups of Fadaeean Khalgh are also under pressure, and whoever is arrested will be executed as an anti-revolutionary.

Continuation of the Iran–Iraq war, unemployment, high prices, hot weather, long cuts of energy, and shortage of food are daily problems of the people. In such an environment, they ask people to identify anti-revolutionaries. People are so involved with their own problems that they pay no attention to such nightly and daily papers and statements.

JULY 13, 1981

Every day they announce that a team house of Mojahedin was discovered, and arms are found there. Then they execute some people for this reason. They declare that they have found bombs at mosques, bridges, and public places and defused them.

The United States announced that their Supreme Court has validated the Algeria Treaty and will free two billion dollars of Iranian deposits. Iraq proclaimed a ceasefire during Ramadan, but Iran did not accept it. Libya and Syria supported the ceasefire during Ramadan. The Iranian prime minister said that their position has not changed and will not accept ceasefire as long as Iraq troops are in Iranian territory.

Candidates for the presidency were announced. Between seventy people, the Guardian Council approved credibility of four - all from the same school of thought. Mohammad Ali Rajaee, the Parveresh deputy of the Parliament, Shaibani, the ex-minister of agriculture, and Askar Ouladi, an MP, are candidates. The media encourages people to vote. They are concerned about the nonparticipation of people.

JULY 27, 1981

On July 24, the election of the president and fifty MPs was done. A few days before the election, Askar Ouladi was faced with an attempted killing. Three candidates granted their votes to Rajaee. Therefore, the election was in favor of Rajaee without any competitors. People were afraid that nonparticipation in the election would make trouble for them, but they voted for miscellaneous candidates; the others did not vote at all.

With all the precautions, there was some unrest by the opposition that resulted in eleven deaths. It was announced that the number of Rajai's votes exceeded Banisadr's votes, which were eleven million. Conditions for the presidency were: being religious, following Imam's line, and being from a deprived group of society. Rajaee had all the conditions.

For the position of prime minister, Bahonar, secretary general of the Islamic Republic Party, and Behzad Nabavi, the government speaker, were nominated.

In *Lomond* newspaper, some intellectuals asked people of the world to pay attention to the situation in Iran, especially to the execution of the opposition that was going on nonstop.

On the day of election, some Iranians outside the country made some useless demonstrations that were short term.

Arrests and executions of Mojahedin Khalgh are going on. Banisadr announced unity with Mojahedin, assumed to be the president, and elected a shadow cabinet. He gave the position of prime minister to Masoud Rajavee, the leader of Mojahedin.

JULY 30, 1981

Yesterday an earthquake measuring seven on the Richter scale moved Kerman once more and killed about five thousand people. Such a disaster for the people of Kerman is making them homeless, and it is really sad.

Yesterday, Banisadr and his prime minister, Masoud Rajavi, fled Iran by an army Boeing jet that was flown by pilot Moezi. They were admitted with refugee status in France. Moezi was the Shah's pilot on his last trip from Iran. He was detained on return. When in power, Banisadr released him with the excuse of the Iran–Iraq war and called him to service.

France granted political refugee status to Banisadr and Rajavi, provided that they have no political activities inside France. At the moment of arrival, journalists and photographers interviewed them. Banisadr said that the whole time he was hiding in Tehran and fled from Mehrabad Airport. Last night his interview was spread by news agencies. Banisadr called himself president and said the presidency of Rajaee invalid.

A few days ago, Mohammad Reza Saadati, a leader

of Mojahedin Khalgh at the start of the Islamic republic who was in prison with the accusation of spying for Russia, was executed. He was sentenced to ten years imprisonment, but the government declared that he took part in the killing of Kachoui, the head of Evin Prison.

The hunting and execution of Mojahedin Khalgh is still going on, and they fight against the regime. Bomb explosions in different parts of the city worry people. A bomb in a cinema killed ten people.

June 26 coincided with the Shah's death anniversary. A ceremony was held for this in Cairo, and a message was sent by Reza Pahlavi, the crown prince. Radio and TV stated that Banisadr had co-ordinated his flight with this day.

An Argentinean airplane that crashed in Russia created rumors that it was carrying arms from Israel to Iran. The government speaker said that Iran rents airplanes for its needs, and this airplane was carrying purchased equipment to Iran. The Islamic Republic of Iran denies any relationship with Israel.

SEPTEMBER 1, 1981

This month the Islamic republic has discovered some team houses of Mojahedin and obtained arms from them, and then again executed the members of Mojahedin Khalgh. The Mojahedin are killing Imam Jomehs, the Pasdarans, and bombing places. The last instance was the bombing of the prime minister's office on August 30 that resulted in killing President Rajaee, Prime Minister Bahonar, and other people. Yesterday it was a holiday for this, along with one week of public mourning. Now two people remain from the council of the presidency; the chair of the Supreme Court and the chairman of Parliament are running the country. An attempted killing of the two did not work.

In an interview in Paris, Banisadr and Masoud Rajavi denied their partnership in the plot and stated that this was the result of cruelty by the government to the people. The chairman of Parliament and the public prosecutor stated that from now on they will act more harshly with the opposition.

The day after the incident which resulted in the killing of the president and the prime minister, the city was at peace. As people hear of more and more killings, they become indifferent.

Last month a small battleship that was delivered to Iran by France was seized by the Azadegan Group, with the leadership of General Aryana and the commandership of Habibollahi. By the mediation of France, the battleship was returned and the seizers were given refugee status. The Islamic republic asked for capture of them in the name of piracy.

The government is facing many problems; the most important of them is the oppression of the opposition. In Delhi, a group of people are on a food strike and asked the world to pay attention to the situation in Iran. The opposition has occupied Iranian embassies in some cities, but is settled by the police.

The United States has released one billion dollars of Iranian deposits; the other one billion dollars will be at the disposal of the committee that is to settle the disputes between Iranian and American companies.

In a statement by the Iranian government about the bombing of the prime minister's office, they said the United States was responsible for that event.

Rationing meat was cancelled due to problems in implementation, but meat is very scarce; the same with chicken and eggs. Dairy is distributed by portion. Seasonal fruits are so expensive that few can afford to buy it.

People are expecting an event or a miracle to change the existing situation. Nothing is stable and accountable, except something unusual.

Night traffic is under the control of the Pasdaran. Mojahedin makes trouble with the arms and uniforms that they have obtained. Some of them confiscate cars.

SEPTEMBER 6, 1981

In continuation of the two-sided murder, Ghodousi, the public prosecutor, was killed in a bomb explosion in his office. After the assassination of President Rajaee and Prime Minister Bahonar, Ghodousi swore that he would have a very harsh confrontation with the opposition and not let them go. Ayatollah Khomeini said, "Kill us. You will not benefit from killing us; we are ready to be sacrificed."

Now Iran is a country of violence. Authorities are not able to save themselves against their enemies. Some of the opposition has penetrated inside their circles, and they are able to plan the right moments in the prime minster and public prosecutor's offices.

A few of the prime minister's staff were arrested in relation with the bombing. It was found that the police commander was among those assassinated. In the first days, they concealed this from the people.

With the internal chaos, the army has made some progress in the war fronts that are exaggerated on the news.

Mehdavi Kani was appointed by Parliament to the prime minister's position. The replacement for the public prosecutor is Mousavi Tabriz.

SEPTEMBER 15, 1981

In the past few days, seventy Mojaheds were executed by the Revolutionary Court. In Tabriz, Ayatollah Madani, a friend of Ayatollah Khomeini, was killed by a bomb along with six people. The bomber was killed as well. It was announced that Kashmiri, the president's secretary, was killed during the bombing in the prime minister's office and was responsible.

Every day Mojahedin demonstrate in the city and kill the Pasdarans. In replacement of Madani, Imam Jomeh Tabriz, Meshkini, the temporary Imam Jomeh Ghom, went to Tabriz. Ayatollah Khomeini said, "No matter how many clergies you kill, we have others to replace them."

The election of the third president will be held on October 2. So far, forty people are nominated. The Guardians Council should approve their competency.

SEPTEMBER 28, 1981

Yesterday the greatest street fight happened. Mojahedin put eight buses on fire, one belonging to the gendarmerie. A minimum of ten people were killed, and a great number wounded. The execution of Mojahedin is going on. Since the dismissal of Bani Sadr, two thousand Mojahedin are killed.

The election of the president is on Friday, October 2. Rumors are that Khamenee, who lost his hand in Jomeh Prayer, will become president.

In a successful attack by the army and Sepah Pasdaran, they were able to break the blockage of Abadan, capture one thousand Iraqis, and obtain a great amount of arms.

Iraq is becoming tired of the war and repeatedly

demands negotiations. Muslim and Arab countries would like to stop the war.

Iranian pilgrims to Mecca made propaganda for the Islamic Republic of Iran, and Saudi police attacked them and arrested and wounded many. This was protested by the Iranian Ministry of Foreign Affairs. In India, Iranians and Iraqis were fighting, which made the Indian government furious.

The Islamic hijab (veil) issue has become serious. In the offices and stores, women without hijab are barred from entering. Hijab means a head scarf, loose and long coat, heavy socks, and flat shoes. It is foreseen that very soon men and women will be separated on the streets, buses, and taxies.

Laying off women with different excuses has started. Their jobs are given to unemployed men, and women are pushed inside their homes.

The president of the Central Bank informed people of the hard economic situation, deficit, and reduction of oil income. The heavy budget that is assigned for war will create great problems for the future government that is going to start in a month's time.

OCTOBER 1, 1981

At 7:00 PM on Tuesday, an airplane crashed near Kahrizak; it killed and wounded many of the soldiers from the war in Khozestan and four army commanders, Falahi, the substitute commander, Namjou, the minister of defense, Ayatollah Khomeini, a representative in the High Council of Defense, Fakouri, the air force commander, and Kolahdouz, the deputy of Sepah Pasdaran. Three days of public mourning were announced for them with a formal funeral ceremony. This was a great loss for the army. They mourned while they were celebrating victory in the war against Iraq. It is not clear whether the crash was due to a technical fault or if it was sabotage. As the airplane crashed on residential area of Kahrizak, some more were killed. So far they have not announced the exact number of victims. The event distracted the attention of people away from the election of the president.

All oppositions banned participation in the election of the president. It is foreseen that the number will be enough for validity of the election.

OCTOBER 11, 1981

At last the third president was elected and got his firman from Ayatollah Khomeini. Seyed Ali Khamenei, Imam Jomeh, got sixteen million votes, 95 percent. He said he will continue the path of the slain president and will not nominate a new cabinet. He is a hard-liner and extremist that received militia training in Libya, and he is a partisan of Moamar Ghadafi, the president of Libya.

The important event of last week was the death of Anvar Sadat, the president of Egypt, by Khaled Islamboli during a march on the October 5 anniversary of the war with Israel. Sadat enemies are hard-liner Muslims that do not like his friendship with the United States.

Americans honored Sadat and three previous presidents participated in the funeral ceremony. For security reason, the ceremony was very simple. Possibly Hosni Mobarak, the vice president, will replace Sadat. He promised to follow the path of Sadat and honor the Camp David Treaty with Israel.

In Egypt, some unrest started. Ayatollah Khomeini triggered them.

Among governments of the world, only Iran and

Libya expressed their happiness with the assassination of Sadat. Arabic countries condemn the terrorism. The United States and European countries support Sadat's substitute.

In his first speech, Seyed Ali Khamenei stated that in case the opposition stops disagreements, he will have nothing to do with them. He is in favor of hard confrontation, and will possibly treat Mojahedin in a harder way.

In the Iran–Iraq war, some progress is being made. Once again, Iraq proposed a peace agreement that is going to be discussed in the High Council of Defense. The Islamic Conference started new tactics for removing differences between Iran and Iraq.

MARCH 15, 1981

The Iranian year is close to the end. The year that passed was very difficult for Iranians. Although hard work had been done to finish the war, it is still going on and wasting financial resources and the life of the younger generation. The slogan is: "War, War, Until Victory."

The Iranian conditions for peace are: unconditional deportation of Iraqi soldiers, payment for war compensation, recognizing Iraq as an aggressor, and the return of all refugees that were sent to Iran. Some delegations from various countries came to Iran to solve the problem of war; they all returned empty-handed.

In Iran, more commodities are rationed. The price of these commodities on the black market by mediators is unaccountable.

Foreign goods are scarce. Spare parts for factories and home appliances are impossible to find. When repair is needed, it is better to put it away.

Whatever free time people have is used for providing minimum requirements for their living. High prices are unbelievable. Some commodity prices have gone up five to six times.

The government controls everything, and there is no room for complaint. People who start complaining are considered anti-revolution and punished. The government sold gold reserves and items in museums and royal palaces.

The oil market is saturated, and the producers are competing to bring the prices down. OPEC members protested Iran, who was the first country that reduced the price of oil. Iranian oil is traded for arms and food with Eastern countries that have good relationships with Iran, and this worries the Free World. If a change happens in Iran, surely it will cause more influence from Russia and the Toudeh Party.

Negotiations with Japan on the commissioning of the petrochemical industry reached a dead end. Completion of the project will meet needs, and it could be a great source of export income. The project is left idle; 15 percent remains incomplete. The government is not able to cover the heavy damages to the site of the project because of the burden of war expenses. The government asked people to help with the coverage of the war requirements. People are mostly unemployed and suffering from inflation. Some profiteers are looting people. Efforts of the government are no good. Most factories are on the verge of a halt because they lack professional staff, financial sources, spare parts, and raw materials. Even those great industries that are nationalized and run by the public sector are not efficient.

Ayatollah Khomeini ordered an investigation of

the situation with prisoners; the number of them is not known. He ordered religious instructions be given to those with political crimes. Those who admit and cooperate can be released.

Recently a few army commanders, who were suspected of a coup d'état were detained. The government trusts Sepah Pasdaran (the guardian corp.) and constantly increases their authorities and privileges. After the murder of Mousa Khiabani and the wife of Masoud Rajavi, the terror activities have accelerated.

Rabani Shirazi, a member of the Guardian Council of the constitution and supervisor of the Constructive Jihad, has been assassinated.

In France, a court was held for trial of those who decided to kill Shapour Bakhtiar (the last prime minister of the Shah). Iran called this court fake and reduced their relationship with France. In the Friday prayer, they chanted "death to France."

There is no welcome ceremony for Norooz (the Iranian New Year). It is recommended that people pay the money for helping war-stricken people.

MARCH 28, 1982

Contrary to a recommendation by the government on ignoring Norooz, when spring arrived, people welcomed it and performed the related ceremonies.

On the second day of the New Year, there was a heavy attack by the Iranians on Iraqi troops; they captured eight thousand Iraqis and some booty, and six hundred kilometers of occupied lands were taken back. There is no correct estimate for loss that occurred to Iranian troops; it is estimated to be between one thousand and ten thousand. The government does not give proper information in this regard.

Foreign agencies do not believe the news given by Iran and Iraqi media. Foreign News Agencies are invited to come to Iran. It was decided to admit those who give real news. The recent victory of Iran may change the destiny of war. Inside, Iraq is at unrest. We have to wait and see what will happen and at what price this damn war will end.

Saddam Hussein declared that he has no territory claim and is ready to withdraw his troops from Iran. The Islamic republic claims war compensation. If foreign authorities help, the war will end in the failure of Iraq, and Iraq would be compelled to pay compensation.

God knows how many youth have lost their lives in this war, and how much vital resources have been spent. If the war is terminated in a respectful manner, there will be a possibility of renovation and provision of facilities for people.

The sale of oil has become a problem. The international oil market is saturated. Iran has to sell oil under OPEC prices which are agreeable to the members of OPEC. The sale of oil is done by clearing method (exchange of goods). In the New Year, fruit and delicacies were plenty in the market, but the prices were so high that purchase was impossible for many. The government tries to control the prices; only items that are rationed have fixed prices, the other commodities are sold in a black market at high prices.

This year the spring weather was unusually cold, and a heavy snowfall closed most roads. Those who went to the northern part of Iran for the New Year holidays were not able to come back.

APRIL 21, 1982

The Iran–Iraq war is still going on and mediation

of different sources does not work. Recently a new event happened. Sadegh Ghotbzadeh, the minister of foreign affairs, supervisor of Radio and Television, and close friend of Ayatollah Khomeini, made a coup d'état attempt on return to Iran. Many groups and persons were involved in the attempt. He confirmed the case in a TV interview and confessed that he wanted to explode Jamaran, a residence of Ayatollah Khomeini. He also said that Ayatollah Shariatmadari was aware of the plot, but he was scared. He promised that he would recognize the attempt if it was successful. Rayshary, the army public prosecutor, said that Ghotbzadeh received five hundred thousand rials from Shariatmadari's son-in-law for the execution of the plot.

Ghotbzadeh and his troops, which numbered from forty to one thousand, are not going be executed quickly because of the information they can provide. It is reported that the CIA, Israel, Socialists (France), Monarchists, and other groups were involved in the plot.

Clergies at Ghom discredited Ayatollah Shariatmadari from religious leadership. The Tehran Bazaar closed because of the discovery of the plot. Sadegh Ghotbzadeh asked the public prosecutor to "kill me fast or make me free." He assumes himself dead. It seems that he cooperated with the regime and disclosed names of his friends.

The son of Shariatmadari in Germany made a statement and said, "My ailing father did not cooperate with anyone." The home of Shariatmadari is surrounded by the Pasdaran and his family and relatives were arrested; the assets at his disposal were confiscated.

Followers of Shariatmadari are asked to get financial

assistance from his office and find another leader for themselves.

The difference between the Islamic republic and Ayatollah Shariatmadari appeared when the constitution was under discussion and he disagreed with Velayat Faghih. After, he was isolated and lived in Ghom under control. He is not allowed to leave the country. The public prosecutor stated that he will be investigated, and in a TV interview, he wished the Shariatmadari's son-in-law had not cooperated with Ghotbzadeh.

With so much courtesy to Ayatollah Khomeini and being his best friend, it was very unbelievable for Ghotbzadeh to plan a coup d'état. It was due to his ambition or his cooperation with enemies of the Islamic republic. Now it is clear that the humbleness in the beginning was fabricated for a certain goal.

It was said that Bazargan and Yazdi were part of the plot, and that was later denied by them in Parliament.

MAY 10, 1982

The story of Shariatmadari is almost forgotten. He appeared on TV and stated that, "I pray to be excused by God for not informing the Islamic Republic about the coup d'état." He asked Ayatollah Khomeini to stop the media from exaggerating the case, because his life was in danger. He disappointed his followers, but outside followers stated that the interview was for saving himself. How could a person in old age who loves his life participate in a dangerous action like this?

After the interview with Ghotbzadeh, Shariatmadari's son-in-law and Jomeh Imam of Gholhak Mosque were interviewed. This imam was disgraced, his religious outfit was taken, and he was dressed in the ordinary.

Once again, the war between Iran and Iraq

accelerated and drew everybody's attention. The Iranian army had a wonderful victory and occupied some important garrisons and set the Iraqi army back to the border. During their return, the Iraqis ruined the two cities of Hovayzeh and Hamid, important strategic stations, and turned them into a hill of dust that was shown on TV. However, no statement was made about freeing Khoramshahr. The Iraqis try not to evacuate the occupied territories; that would be proof of their failure. It has been nineteen months of war that resulted in thousands of Iranian lives lost and a waste of financial sources for the two parties.

Yesterday a powerful bomb exploded in front of the Syrian embassy, ruined a four-story building, and wounded some passersby. The reason was support of Syria by the Islamic republic against Iraq.

In recent weeks, a few more team houses of Mojahedin were discovered and about fifty or more Mojahedin were killed. The government stated that Mojahedin are finished, but still, terrorist acts are committed by them. Their center for their activities is in Paris, where they distribute their statements.

MAY 19, 1982

It is claimed that the Islamic republic has given freedom and pride to women, and their prestige has gone up. However, they hate women who do not observe Islamic hijab, and they are hardly encountered.

On the entry of every shop, ministry, park, bus, and taxi is written: "Entry of women without veil is forbidden." Every wall in the city bears slogans against women without hijab. These are some of these slogans:

- Woman without hijab is a prostitute.

- Woman without hijab is offering herself.
- Woman without hijab is an agent of imperialism.
- Husbands of women without hijab have no zeal.
- Having no hijab means mental slavery.
- Being without hijab is a sign of a mental disorder.
- Woman's hijab is her rifle pit.
- My sister, your hijab is more colorful than blood of martyrs.
- Support martyrs with your hijab.
- Woman without hijab, shame on you, beware of martyrs' blood.
- Woman's hijab is a hard blow on the mouth of Super Powers.

The overcoat of women should be dark and loose, so that her body is fully hidden underneath. She should have a head scarf and heavy trousers in a dark color, and should not shake hands with men. Her voice and laugh should not be heard. Hezbollah will treat women without hijab in a very harsh manner.

In employment advertisements, men are preferred to women. Women are recommended to have part-time jobs and receive half of the salary. If a married woman quits her job, her husband receives a 40 percent raise. Cleansing Councils dismiss women with minor excuses. In girls' schools, when the teacher is a woman, girls have to wear hijab. The minister of education said, "Boys and girls should be trained in different ways."

Men are allowed to marry four wives; having a concubine is easy and is recommended to men who are well off. They encourage youths to marry wives of martyrs so that they are not left alone. The marriage of girls at young ages is common. It is clear that the presence of women in society has diminished.

By the office of Forbidden Fighting, they inspect every office and of private sector to make sure that women in the working place are considering their hijab, otherwise the director of the business will be condemned to a lash or cash penalty. Girls are lashed at the office of Fighting Forbidden or their ears are pulled. If a person is at the Fighting Forbidden a second time, his workplace will be closed. This is a good excuse for companies not to employ women.

From nine years old, girls have to dress the Islamic way. Divorce is the right of the husband, who can easily divorce his wife. Islamic authorities encourage marriage and give facilities to those who like to marry, such as loans, permits for buying household furniture, refrigerators, and ovens that are very scarce and have very high prices.

Where the presence of men and women are required, they provide different seats for them, so as not to mingle. They try to separate them in buses and taxis. When in formal situations where the presence of a woman is required, the husband may replace his wife, and it is acceptable. If a man is outside the country, his wife is allowed to join him. If a woman is outside the country, her husband may not travel by that excuse, because he may easily find a replacement for her. Women are not allowed to wear high-heeled shoes that make noise when they walk. All women are in uniform. Having ornaments is forbidden. Every newcomer will see what an Islamic society looks like.

Before women were employed for serving in the army; now they are hired for different paramilitary groups to serve at the rear of the fronts and help their brothers if they are Basij and Sepah.

They have decided to train male nurses for men, and gynecologists are only women. When universities are open, the male and female classes are separated; for girls they hire female professors. After four years, they hold an examination for sending students abroad. Girls are allowed in specific fields. Jobs that remain for women are teaching, nursing, and office works. In the upper scale of management, there are no women. Women are given privileges for early retirement. In the high unemployment situation, priority is given to men. Each woman should find a man to support her. In industries, women receive lower wages. Women from minorities and foreign women are compelled to wear the Islamic veil.

MAY 26, 1982

On May 24, 1982, the Iranian army returned Khoramshahr from Iraq. After about eighteen months, the city was occupied by Iraq. This city is very important from a strategic viewpoint and for access to Shatolarab. Iraqis had a very strong army station in the city. In the fighting, about eighteen thousand Iraqi soldiers were captured by Iranian troops. Iranians celebrated the victory in every city. People showed the same enthusiasm when the Shah left Iran. Yesterday the prime minister went to Khoramshahr and prayed in Jome Masjid. This city was one of the most beautiful cities in Iran; now it is a ruined place.

Iranian victory worries the neighboring Arab countries; they are afraid that the Iranian army is going to further occupy Iraq. Iranian authorities emphasize that they do not intend to occupy the other's territories, but they chant some slogans about occupying Baitolmoghadas in Israel and Karbala in Iraq, which causes worry for countries in the Persian Gulf area. They try to make a unity between themselves to be prepared for a possible attack by Iran. Ayatollah Khomeini stated that if the small countries do not follow U.S. policy and join Iran, they will be safe.

A country that is a target of propaganda of the Islamic regime is Egypt, which clearly supports Saddam Hussein and sends arms to him. The United States warned Egypt about sending U.S. arms to Iraq. Now it is too late for Iraq to use these arms to the benefit of its army.

After Khoramshahr, it will be time for freeing Ghasreshirin and other cities. As the Iraqi army suffered heavy damages, they have only one route, which is to accept their failure, pay compensation, and unconditionally evacuate Iranian territory. Foreign news agencies accepted that the victory in Khoramshahr was a huge defeat for Iraq. There is no information about the loss of lives in Iranian troops. Whatever it was, they were ready for it. With the position of surrendering by Iraqis, it was less than what was expected.

JUNE 14, 1982

The main incident that happened and made the world busy was the attack of Israel on South Lebanon and stations of the Palestine Liberation Front. In the early days, the main part of Lebanon was occupied by Israel. Israel declared a ceasefire, and Syria and the Liberation Front of Palestine accepted it, but Israel kept up its progress. Today they occupy some ministries in the capital city and are very close to the palace of the president. Israel stated that they do not intend to occupy

Lebanon but like to have a friendly government to keep its borders immune.

Occupied lands were submitted to Major Saad Haddad that previously separated part of the Lebanese land. Syria had heavy damages and the stations of Palestinians are completely demolished and people homeless. The Islamic Republic of Iran attacked Israel harshly and said it is ready to declare Jihad to help Syria and free the south of Lebanon. For this purpose, they allocated a budget and collected some volunteers. As going to Syria is possible only through Iraq, they asked for a transit permit. Iraq used this opportunity and said they would withdraw soldiers from Iran and unilaterally will enforce a ceasefire; they are ready to refer compensation. Iran did not accept the conditions, and they are insisting on the fall of Hussein and the Ba'ath Party and the establishment of an Islamic republic in Iraq.

The United States pretends not to agree with Israel, but it is not believed that such a great attack could take place without consultation of the United States.

Arabic countries oppose the action of Israel, but they did nothing to prevent that attack. Maybe they like to have a moderate government in Lebanon to prevent Palestinian aggression.

More than any other country, the Islamic Republic of Iran shows sympathy with people in South Lebanon, but does not have a land truck available, and therefore can do nothing.

The Amal Movement, which is partisan to the Islamic Republic of Iran, had heavy losses. Suda and Sydan that were a gathering shelter for Palestinians are totally demolished and their fighting power is diminished. The United States wants to assign some lands in the Gaza Strip for the homeless Palestinians and give them autonomy. If Israel can fully occupy Lebanon and establish a Western-friendly government and scatter Palestinians there, it would be a new power balance in the Middle East.

Russia, with ten years of cooperation and a friendship treaty with Syria, has not entered in on the plot. They only made a statement in favor of Syria and Palestine. Fighting between Israel and Lebanon caused relative peace on the Iran–Iraq war front. So far, no final solution is found for ending the war. The amount of compensation that was decided for the parties is 150 billion dollars. Some Arab countries have agreed to help with the compensation to Iran.

The next condition of Iran is the dismissal of Saddam Hussein, which is not an easy job. His fall will worry all Arab countries. Syria, who pretended to be a friend of Iran, condemns the attack of Iran on Iraq. Iran pretends it will occupy Baghdad, but so far has done nothing beyond its borders because of a fear of the reaction of Arab countries. Mediation of international organizations, non-alliance countries, and Islamic countries was not successful in ending the war between Iran and Iraq. At the meeting in Cuba, the non-obligatory countries insisted on having their next meeting in Baghdad.

JUNE 17, 1982

For one week Iran has made hard attacks on Iraqi territory. About one hundred thousand army personnel were called for service. This is the biggest war involvement since the Second World War. The United States and Russia pulled out of the war and declared neutrality. The attack of Iran on Iraq had a great reaction and subdued the attack of Israel against the Palestine

Freedom Front. Iraqi airplanes bombarded a few cities in Iran, including Hamedan, and came close to Tehran a few times.

Israel announced that if Iran decides to come to Baytolmoghadas, they will destroy them before any action takes place.

Ayatollah Khomeini named one Friday during Ramadan as the "Day of Ghods," and a demonstration was done with the goal of the occupation of Baytolmoghas. It is possible that this phase also takes time and will become an erosion war. Now the future of this war is unclear and depends on which party is able to find a new supporter. Surely some more people will be killed and resources wasted.

The Islamic republic minister of foreign affairs announced that the dismissal of Saddam Hussein is not a condition for ending the Iran–Iraq war; it is only a recommendation to people in Iraq. On the same day, the other authorities announced that the dismissal and trial of Saddam Hussein was their condition, and an Islamic republic government was acceptable to Iran in order to liberate Baytolmoghadas via Iraq.

JULY 10, 1982

Iraq unilaterally evacuated the mainland of Iran. The evacuated cities are totally destroyed, including Ghasreshin which was a beautiful city. The only remains of the city are a mosque and customs office.

The reason brought about for occupation of Basra is that the city was the place where Iran was a target of far-reaching canons from Iraq.

About 180,000 land mines were planted at the border lines of Iran and Iraq. So far, Iranians have neutralized five thousand of them. Iraq proposed to decide about the aggressor, and the amount of compensation is referred to International Arbitration, the United Nations, and a meeting of non-alliance Islamic countries. The Iranian government accepted none of them, and in advance, declared that it will not accept the view of the Security Council. The same three conditions that were mentioned before should be realized.

Iran is involved with war damages that no compensation can cover. Iranian diplomats also believe in the idea of conquering Iraq and going from there for freedom of Baytolmoghadas. Israel promised to bombard all water and power establishments in Iran if they try to come into Israel.

Now the war between Israel and Palestine has entered a very crucial stage. Israel insists on the departure of Palestinians from Lebanon. Palestinians are surrounded by Israel, and their water and power is cut. The United States promised to send ships for evacuating Palestinians and dispatched gunmen to supervise their safe departure.

The Palestine Freedom Front has faced great human and financial losses, and their gathering centre is ruined. Israel has taken all their heavy artilleries. Very important negotiations are going on for stopping Israel from attacking South Lebanon and killing Palestinians that are surrounded. Russia, a good friend of Palestine, has done nothing in this regard. In its first attempt, Syria lost some airplanes and tanks. Israel warned them to leave Lebanese lands and a government will rise to power that is a friend of Israel. The solution for Palestine will affect the decision of the Islamic Republic of Iran on helping Palestine and fighting with Israel. There are some rumors that Israel and the Palestine Liberal

Organization may formally recognize each other's sovereignty.

Last week, Ayatollah Sadoughi, the close friend of Ayatollah Khomeini, was assassinated during Jomeh prayer. A great mourning was held for him and one day was a public holiday. The terrorist was killed as well.

SEPTEMBER 1, 1982

It is three months since the attack of the Iranian army on Iraq, but no considerable progress has been made. By persistence of Iran, the conference of non-alliance countries that was planned to be held in Baghdad changed its place to India. The pressure of Israel on Palestine accelerated to the degree that they left Lebanon and scattered in Arabic countries, but they stated that they will continue their fighting with Israel. The host countries will prevent them from military activities, and the fact they have lost their artillery and their army is scattered makes it unbelievable that they can maintain their previous status.

Ayatollah Khomeini instructed all Iranian laws to be converted to Islamic laws, and the courts do not act on any law except those Islamic laws. There are no anti-Islamic laws among the Iranian laws, but all of them do not comply exactly with Islamic laws. After this firman, Parliament ratified the bill of Ghesas (revenge). From now on, the Ghesas punishment will rule.

Ayatollah Khomeini ordered Ayatollah Montazeri to divide dead lands, confiscated lands, and those that have no owner among farmers in order for the country to reach self-sufficiency in agriculture.

Due to the bombardment on Khark Island or other reasons, the shortage of oil became a problem again. Streets in Tehran that used to have heavy traffic are now isolated and the air has become unpolluted. The number of buses and taxis is not enough. Cigarettes are sold for forty tomans a pack on the black market. Some people from committees that were selling home appliances in the black market are trapped. Commodities are plenty in the black market. The Government tries to prevent them, but it is not possible; people are under pressure and there is no control. Inflation and unemployment is hard on people.

The government has decided to let the parents of students that are receiving educational assistance go abroad. This caused many people to request using this facility, but the issue of visas for these people was not arranged, and it was stopped again.

DECEMBER 5, 1982

Due to the cruelty of the Revolutionary Courts and the government staff, Ayatollah Khomeini issued a nine-article firman in which confiscation of properties and the arrest of people without having a verdict from the court is forbidden. A commission was held to investigate the complaints. It was decided that they return the properties that were taken from people without good reason. They have to stop searching the private status of people and spying on them and not listen to telephone calls. They have to stop searching the correspondence of people and pardon those who worked in the ex-regime and are ready to work with the Islamic Republic of Iran.

On the execution of the firman, a few public prosecutors were dismissed, and people were finding peace of mind. The other case that helped people was freeing the consumption of oil and gas that was now produced domestically. Because of the world price of oil, which caused differences between OPEC members, it is more economical to sell the oil inside the country.

The other instructions by Khomeini were about entry examinations of the universities. In ministries and in universities, they chose the individuals they like for the excuse of ideology tests so complicated that even intellectuals could not answer. Among the staff of choosing committees were prejudiced individuals and Hezbollah men that did not like the intellectuals. This procedure of Paksazi (purification) Committees and Islamic Associations caused intellectuals and experts to be laid off. Now they are distressed for they cannot manage a society with many problems. Now they feel a need for experts. Some missions are working on the return of experts, and they are ready to give them any guarantee to come back and start working. It was announced that those who escaped to foreign countries would be reimbursed with their properties that were confiscated.

At Friday prayer, Rafsanjani spoke about Khoms (one-fifth) of deposits to be taken from the people as the Islamic tax and calculated that it would be a huge figure. This meaningless statement caused people to withdraw their deposits from banks, and it made a catastrophe for the government. The statement was somehow modified, but people lost their confidence. It is not anticipated that they return the deposits in the short time ahead.

Last month universities and colleges were reopened, but they made it hard for students, and many of them were not admitted. Ayatollah Khomeini instructed the dissolution of choosing bodies and simplification of tests. It was announced that those who failed ideology tests and were deprived from entry into universities and offices could take the tests again. They hoped to reduce complaints this way.

Days before Norooz on the 22 Bahman anniversary of the Revolution, all Iranian ceremonies were performed for Norooz, and they claimed the day being the Iranian New Year. They tried to prevent people from having Norooz celebrations.

Iraq received support from other countries and bombarded the southern cities of Iran. Due to the conspiracy of oil consumer countries, OPEC faced a severe crisis, which resulted in the fall of oil prices in the world market from thirty-four dollars to twenty-eight dollars a barrel. It is possible it could go down more. The Islamic Republic of Iran that was relying on oil income for war, renovation of ruins, and welfare of the people lost a big amount of income. The conference of non-alliance countries of 130 countries worked hard to terminate the Iran–Iraq war faced resistance from the Iranian side and gave it up.

After the eight articles of Ayatollah Khomeini's firman, some women tried to remove their hijab, which ended in hard punishment. A public prosecutor announced that women without hijab would end up in Evin Prison. Then Hezbollah started to punish women. Women without Islamic hijab will face harsh reactions. It is likely that the firman has lost its spirit, and instead a new bureaucracy is established in the country.

On the revolution's anniversary (22 Bahman), it was announced that the borders are opened and people may travel abroad. The day after, there was big rush to the passport office. They had to close the doors and ask people to send their applications by mail. So far nobody was able to use this facility. The entry of foreign exchange to Iran is allowed. Whoever imports foreign exchange will own it, and may do whatever they wish with the money. They expected big amounts of foreign money imported to the country to provide for foreign trips of their friends, but it did not work, and there is no news about opening of borders.

APRIL 19, 1982

By bombardment of two oil wells in the Persian Gulf (Norooz and Ardeshir), it is about one month that oil has been leaking into the Persian Gulf and endangering the life of sea animals and creatures. Passage of vessels is difficult, and provision of water for countries around the Gulf is getting impossible. Iran and Iraq did not agree on a temporary ceasefire in order for Iran to be able to repair the damages to oil wells and oil leaks in the Gulf. With heavy loss and waste of resources, Iran and Iraq are still involved in a war. In Alfajr 1 and 2 wars, both countries claimed heavy damages to the other party.

MAY 2, 1982

The Islamic Republic of Iran started a very severe confrontation against the Tudeh Party, who were their ally in the beginning of the revolution. First they arrested some of the leaders of the party and then arranged TV interviews with them. They all confessed to being traitors and being attached to Russia. Each of these crimes could end up in execution of the leaders of the Tudeh Party. Kianoori, the secretary general, and Behazin, a member of the Central Committee, made statements about the Tudeh Party's treacherous activities that amazed the listeners. The Tudeh Party during the Dr. Mosaddegh era proved its disloyalty. Today the leaders disclosed forty years of obedience to Russia. It is not clear what policy is behind this show. If they are executed, nobody would protest. The revelation was made the day before on May 1, World Labor Day, to disappoint their members in political activities.

AUGUST 6, 1982

The Valfajr 3 war caused many victims from both sides. The slogan by the Islamic Republic of Iran was: "As long as a child is living, we will fight." Between the powers, fighting is started, and fighting against the Hojatie Group has been disclosed and caused resignation of two ministers.

Yesterday, Mordad 14 (August 5), the anniversary of the constitution, a great silent demonstration was held in Tehran with many participants, which was far from expectations. After four years of an Islamic republic, people showed tendencies toward a constitutional regime. This was the first quiet demonstration with too many people. For hours the roads were blocked, and the government showed no reaction.

The Hojatieh Group that claimed power in the Islamic republic has gone back with a reaction by Ayatollah Khomeini and said they will stop activities not to make any dispersion.

Marine Commander Nakhoda Afzali was arrested and underwent trial. He had no responsibility for a long time.

FEBRUARY 14, 1983

On February 11, the Islamic republic has now been ruling for five years. They celebrated the case very widely and many programs performed on the radio and the TV. Newspapers published the gains with some messages from

Ayatollah Khomeini. He made some recommendations to the authorities and asked them not bother people and to try to solve their problems. The situation in the offices is terrible, and they encounter very impolite people. It is like they have forgotten the recommendations of their leader. Nothing is accomplished in the government offices except disappointing people.

During celebrations of the Fajr Decade, fighting between Iran and Iraq accelerated. Defenseless people are living under bombs. Mediations did not work and each party insists on its own stand. There is no hope for the end of this war, at least before they finish their artillery.

The international situation is not good. Lebanon is on the verge of separation. War between Muslims and Christians ruined this beautiful country.

Opposition to the Islamic republic outside of the country announced that the twenty-second day of Bahman (day of revolution) was a day of protest. They asked people not go out of their homes, but the streets were crowded and Hezbollah made the demonstration.

General Ovaisi was assassinated in Paris. The Islamic republic expressed happiness for his murder and said that the murder be attributed to the Islamic republic.

Youri Andriof, the president of Russia, passed away and Cherminov, a seventy-year-old man, replaced him. There is no hope of any change in the policy of Russia.

The trial of the Tudeh Party leaders ended with the terrible confessions that they made. Three of them in the army section were executed, and the rest condemned to confinement, which is minor compared with the crimes they have committed. Maybe there were some considerations in regard to the north neighbor.

MARCH 16, 1983

The last Wednesday of the year, which is very special for Iran, was interrupted by the Pasdaran hostility. They claim prevention of superstition.

The war between Iran and Iraq reached a new dimension. Iran complained that Iraq has released a chemical bomb on Iranian soldiers. Some of these soldiers were sent abroad for treatment. Physicians of Red Cross confirmed that Iraq used chemical bombs.

Majnoun Island, with worthy oil wells, belonged to Iraq and is occupied by Iran. Both parties suffered heavy loss. Iraq held a conference of the leaders of Arab countries and asked hard action against Iran. All Arab countries, except Libya and Syria who are friends of Iran, condemned Iran and stated that if Iran does not negotiate, they will support Iraq.

This year the Iranian New Year had no happiness. People were somehow engaged with their problems. High prices are terrible and they are continuing. People are sad and disappointed. About five hundred thousand youths are at war fronts, which is a big worry for many people. They do not have the spirit for the New Year. The New Year bonus is only one Bahar Azadi gold coin for those with a monthly salary less than seven thousand tomans. This was an element for stagnancy.

The Islamic regime says we have no New Year. Our New Year is when the war is ended. On April 2, the day of the Islamic republic election may come. Very wide propaganda is going on, and they are trying to show a free election.

Year 1362 (1983/84) is close to the end; a year with many unpleasant events. Now at the beginning of a New Year, we can look forward to better days and the end of war.

MARCH 21, 1985

Every New Year we regret the past New Year. Iranians started their New Year under bombardment, alarm, and darkness. Every moment they were expecting the fall of a bomb on their heads. So far many cities have been bombarded and industrial establishments, such as atomic stations, the petrochemical complex, a pipe-making factory, and refineries, are hit by bombs. Warnings by Iraq cause people to leave their homes. Almost every night Tehran is hit by bombs, and the alarms sound many times. Iran aimed four earth-to-earth missiles to border cities of Iraq, such as Basra. A hard ground fight is going on between Iran and Iraq, and both parties claim victory. It is certain that thousands of Iranian soldiers are vanished in the marshes of Hovayzeh, and some Iraqis are captured by Iranians. Iraq announced that the Iranian sky is a war zone, all foreign airlines cancelled their flights, and the foreign nationals were sent to their countries through special methods. Mehrabad Airport is crowded with passengers who leave Iran. Internal flights are also cancelled, and people leave the provinces by bus or private car. Efforts of the United Nations and other international organizations and non-alliance countries for a ceasefire do not work.

MARCH 30, 1985

Will God damn war and those who start war? It is more than twenty days since Tehran and other cities have been under the attack of bombs and start their nights with alarms. Most bombs are dropped on residential areas. Iranians do not announce the target of bombs and the number of victims.

To revenge the attacks so far, six earth-to-earth missiles have been dropped on Baghdad, which caused heavy damages to human beings and financial sources that worried people in Iraq.

Ceasefire conditions are different for the two parties. Iran wants the stop of attacks on ships, airplanes, and cities, and they will stop missile attacks on Iraqi cities, but they would like to continue ground fighting.

Iraq does not have enough human resources in the fronts and does not like the proposed method of ceasefire; it wants the war negotiated totally and in every aspect.

Mediation of the United Nations and non-alliance countries is useless. Rajive Gandehi, the secretary general of non-alliance countries, has done some negotiations with leaders of the two countries, the object of which is not clear.

Attack on oil tankers in the Persian Gulf caused problems for Iran, and they faced shortages in provision of arms. Recently Iran signed a treaty with China to buy arms; China's arms are not modern.

Countries are curious about the source of ground missiles that are aimed at Baghdad. Iran claims that they are produced domestically. It is said that these are missiles that Russia sold to Libya, and they made them available to Iran.

Peace conditions proposed by Iran are the toppling of Saddam Hussein, payment of 320 billion dollars compensation, and retreat of two hundred thousand Iraqi soldiers to their own country. So far these conditions are not agreed to.

At the ground battle in the marshes of Hour and Hoveyzeh, Iran progressed in Iraqi lands and left many casualties, but declared that it is preparing for another attack on Iraq. Iraq stated that if Iran does not agree with a ceasefire, it will reinforce attacks.

It seems that war is going on and people are suffering the results. With that many problems, can we be optimistic?

SEPTEMBER 24, 1985

My life is aimless and hopeless. It has been six years that the bombardments and news on killing people have disappointed me. The most ridiculous thing that you may hear is that they are celebrating the war's birthday. The sixth anniversary of the war is celebrated.

The academic year started with hard encounters for women with the wrong hijab. Ramadan motorcycle riders made it difficult for people. Fear from these irresponsible people caused the isolation of women.

Khark Island, which was not involved in the war, is now heavily damaged, and Iran's export reached minimum level and is busy with sea fighting. Iran confiscated the vessels that carry Iraqi oil in the Hormoz Strait. Shortage of foreign currency resulted in the cut of three hundred dollars of foreign currency for the traveler and they ask 10.000 Tomans deposit for travelling abroad, which makes travelling abroad very difficult.

The Islamic regime said if it cannot export oil, it will not let oil go out of the Hormoz Strait. The price of oil is declining, and there is oil surplus in the market. OPEC is almost dissolved. Every oil-producing country goes its own way. Economic pressure, unemployment, stagnation, and continuous power cuts affect all economic aspects.

It has been a long time since the president was

elected, but there is no news about choosing a prime minister and a new cabinet.

Last night a bomb exploded in Friday prayer, and a few people were killed. The event was directly on air, and the sound of terrified people was heard. It is not clear who was behind the attack. At the same time, an air attack by Iraq started and the explosion of the bomb was lost in the chaos.

New Year (1365) March 21, 1986

In the long time that I did not follow my notes, nothing has changed ("War, War Till Victory"). There is no sign of war ending, and no sign of victory. Iran has occupied Favo Island. Iraqis say they will take it back, and we have surrounded Iranian troops.

The sudden fall of oil prices made the provision of war expenses and passing the countries affairs very difficult. Every day they invite new forces to join the fight. Ayatollah Khomeini has invited women to join the troops. Women who were ready to go to the fields marched with full Islamic cover in the streets.

This year, the New Year was celebrated more than previous years. Radio and TV of the Islamic regime joined the celebration. Winter was mild, but by springtime, snow and cold surprised people in Tehran and in the provinces.

November 1, 1986

Nothing new has happened. War is the main subject. Sometimes it comes down and then goes up again. At the moment, the situation is favorable to Iran and has attracted views of the world. Recently a big chaos happened about sale of American arms to Iran, which for a while made the foreign media busy. Ronald

Reagan disregarded the regulations set by Congress about the prohibition of the sale of arms to Iran, and he made secret deals with Iran that resulted in the freedom of American hostages in Lebanon. If the case was not disclosed, maybe more hostages could have been freed. The case made more trouble in the United States than in Iran.

Some Iranian MP asked who negotiated with the United States. Ayatollah Khomeini interfered and said, "Such questions will cause dispersion." Two security advisors of the White House were dismissed and different committees started investigation of the case of selling arms to Iran. Every day new events are disclosed. At last a high committee by Congress reasoned that the minister of justice, a member of the cabinet, may not observe neutrality.

Newspapers in the United States went so far that President Reagan called their actions like a dance of sharks in a sea of blood. Israel is also involved in the delivery of arms by order of Reagan. It is said fourteen months of negotiations were going on, and then it was disclosed that the case started from the beginning of the revolution. All Iranian authorities deny having any connection or negotiations in this case.

At Tehran Friday prayer, Imam said, "In case the United States gives back Iranian arms that are paid for by the Shah's regime, we will make our relationship normal." The foreign minister said except for Israel and South Africa, we should have a relationship with the other countries. Reagan tried hard to prove that having a relationship with Iran is necessary for the United States. At the present time, his political situation is not favorable. It is possible that the case of Watergate repeats around him as well. His foreign policy and international credibility are damaged. U.S. allies and Arabic countries are getting disappointed. While the United States encouraged European countries not to sell arms to Iran, it was secretly giving arms to Iran to keep the war between Iran and Iraq alive.

Recently, Lark Terminal, which was ready for the export of oil, was bombarded by Iraq. For the long flight to Lark, Saudi Arabia helped Iraq. This case affected the relationship between Iran and Saudi Arabia that was recently improved. Iran has provided a huge army by Basij (partisans) to dispatch them to the front lines. Iran has expressed many times that the war between Iran and Iraq is going to end soon, but Russia and France keep on providing the most advanced arms to Iraq in order to support the country.

Recently the relationship between Iran and France has improved, and France paid thirty million dollars from their debt to Iran from the Shah's time. At present, the financial state of Iran is getting somehow better.

Italian TV showed a disgusting film about Iran which caused trouble in the relations between the two countries. Iran protested the case, and Italy reasoned that it has no control over TV programs. The BBC is making trouble as usual and exaggerates the sale of arms to Iran by the United States. In the meantime, they are negotiating an important treaty with Iran for the sale of Land Rover cars.

The economic situation is unsettled, and the prices are going up regularly. Dispute among the authorities is so acute that the public has become aware of it. One of the siblings of Ayatollah Montazeri is accused of murder and keeping illegal arms. Later it was found that he was the person who disclosed the arms sale by United States to Iran. For a few days, Ayatollah Montazeri disappeared, and then everything turned back to normal and the accused person was released on bail.

Iran rejects negotiation with the U.S. security advisor of Reagan that visited with a forged passport and negotiated with security authorities. Iran is insisting the purchase of U.S. arms is done through international mediators. Rumors are that part of the money from the sale of arms to Iran has gone to the warriors of Nicaragua, which was forbidden by the U.S. Congress. It is good feedback for international media, and every day a new case of abuse is disclosed.

In Iran, one million women are trained for war activities. This is a sign of paying attention to women power. To go to the field with hijab is a difficult job, but they made it possible.

Special forces for preventing prohibited actions are not very active in the streets, and fear for women has diminished. They threaten women who wear their hijabs improperly with sending them to camps and exile, but it never happens.

FEBRUARY 13, 1986

The Iran–Iraq war reached a very critical stage. Iran attacked Baghdad and Basra and has taken many hostages and toppled many airplanes. Iraq has bombarded residential areas in the cities.

The United Nations and Security Council demanded an urgent stop to this savage war. The scandal of the arms sale by the United States to Iran is continuing. It is said that the CIA has given wrong information to Iran and Iraq so that none of them reach a victory, and U.S. arms are used as usual. Russia, who was declaring neutrality in the war between Iran and Iran in a statement, declared that it will continue supply of arms to Iraq and it does not like an Iranian victory in this war. It seems that this war will continue until the two countries are completely vanished.

The Islamic government managed to repair the power stations that were bombarded by Iraq and reduced the darkness hours. The government asked people to take part in the war.

AUGUST 3, 1986

Sometimes I think time goes fast. It has been months that I did not write, because I do not like to talk about catastrophes and unpleasant events.

Two terrible events happened last week. One was strong floods in major cities of Iran that destroyed homes and made people homeless. It was an unusual rain in the summertime, and it flooded fourteen cities, including North Tehran. They were busy with clean up when the second disaster happened. Two Iranian pilgrims in Mecca were demonstrating and giving slogans, meant to get rid of non-Muslims. A confrontation happened between police and the pilgrims and about four hundred Iranians were killed. This was unusual for a Mecca pilgrimage.

In Tehran, Hezbollah occupied the embassies of Saudi Arabia, Kuwait, and France and took diplomats of Saudi Arabia hostage. Dimensions of this event were very wide and reflected in the world media. Iranians showed their anger in a demonstration and showed hatred towards the United States and Saudi Arabia. The authorities promised to take revenge.

The situation in the Persian Gulf is critical, and warships of the United States, Russia, France, and England are gathered there. The United States committed itself to escort oil tankers of Kuwait. One oil tanker was damaged in hitting a mine and an American helicopter crashed. The United States is distressed because its allies refrain from collecting mines. It is possible that a war between Iran and the United States will start in the Persian Gulf.

Ground fighting between Iran and Iraq continues. After a while, the Security Council made a statement about a ceasefire and asked the parties to go back to their international border lines. The statement was acceptable by Iraq, but Iran did not accept it. Iran promised to stop hitting vessels in the Persian Gulf if Iraq stopped attacking Iranian ships. Iraq said it will start attacking Iranian ships if Iran does not comply with the Security Council statement.

Warnings are going on from every side. The United States said if Iran attacks oil tankers, they will destroy the missile bases. It is a mental fight; every moment there is possibility of shooting the first bullet to start world war three in the Persian Gulf. Every day people face a new crisis; they do not have time to forget the first disaster, and then the second one starts.

The government started a severe fight against high prices and hoarding that caused dissatisfaction of the people. The punishments are slashing, cash penalties, and in rare cases, execution. This caused the prices to go up in the black market. Goods offered for sale have poor quality, but the sellers are rather scared. A few fruit and vegetable markets that did not follow the rules are closed.

SEPTEMBER 9, 1986

War in the Persian Gulf has become serious. All Arab countries and the United States dispatched mine-sweeping vessels and warships to the Persian Gulf. After almost a week, Iraq started to attack Iranian oil tankers and bombard Iranian oil ports, and it has in mind to stop oil export by Iran and improve their own oil export.

Iran and Iraq both asked the U.N. secretary general to mediate in the war. So far Iran has not agreed with a ceasefire and start of negotiation and insists on identification of the aggressor.

Libya who was a friend of Iran, has reconciled with the United States, and they started a diplomatic relationship. So far the killing of Iranians in Mecca is on the table and causes serious disputes between Iran and Saudi Arabia and Muslim countries that support Saudi Arabia.

Iran dispatched more troops to the war front and said it will continue fighting until its wishes are fulfilled. If recommendations by the secretary general of the United Nations are not accepted by Iran, the United Nations will prohibit the sale of arms to Iran by its members. Iran does not care, because from beginning of the war, they provided the required arms through the black market.

Sepah Pasdaran is giving women a hard time. They insist on black color for the outfit of women. In Moharam (mourning month), everybody should wear black to make the city sad. In view of Sepah Pasdaran, black is the main color. It seems that they do not know any other color except black.

APRIL 12, 1988

The reason for not taking any notes for a long time was that 120 missiles attacked Tehran, and people, including my family, evacuated the city. We came back after a short stop, but it started again. Then we went to Isfahan and returned after ten days. Coming and going continues. It is one week since we are settled in a villa at a village near Shahsavar that missiles cannot reach. My grandchildren are going to the village school, and we are waiting to see what will happen.

The subject that attracted the foreign media was the use of chemical bombs by Iraq in a village named Halabche which was occupied by the Iranians. In this chemical bombardment, more than five thousand people were killed in a terrible way, and thousands were wounded. The Islamic regime made big propaganda and invited journalists to view the scene and sent the report all over the world. Many countries condemned Iraq. Saddam Hussein has threatened that he will use chemical bombs on Tehran. The Islamic regime is busy training people to face chemical bombs.

Negotiations by representatives of the United Nations and its secretary general did not work. Iran and Iraq did not change their minds. Iraq wants implementation of the statements by the Security Council, and Iran wants condemnation and punishment of the aggressor.

War has caused financial and administrative damages to the government, and they asked the people's help to provide for expenses of the war. Fear of the attack of missiles causes great loss to the industries.

The government has decided to raise the price of air tickets for those who would like to go abroad. They have to pay it in American dollars, which is seventeen times more than the existing price. This is a barrier to business and tourist trips and can be used only by those with plenty of money. The new decision affected other services and caused the acceleration of prices. In this environment, working and making money is difficult, and there is no light at the end of the tunnel.

The Islamic regime sends soldiers to the front,

and Iraq answers with missiles. Due to last year's demonstrations in Saudi Arabia that resulted in the killing of five hundred people, Saudi Arabia announced that it will not allow more than five thousand Iranian pilgrims. Ayatollah Khomeini answered that we will dispatch 150,000 pilgrims. It is possible that another confrontation will happen between the two countries.

Abduction of a Kuwaiti airplane and its emergency landing in Mashad caused problems between Iran and Kuwait, and now the plane has landed in Cyprus.

JULY 19, 1988

An important accident happened. An Iranian airplane was attacked by Vincent American Warship and crashed in the Persian Gulf waters; 290 passengers were killed. The incident reflected widely in the world media and the United States was compelled to beg pardon, and said it was the fault of Iran who created the crisis in the Persian Gulf and caused interference with the United States. All international organizations and the Security Council admitted that Iran was right.

Suddenly at 2:00 PM yesterday, the radio announced that Iran has unconditionally accepted Statement 598 by the Security Council. Iran strongly and repeatedly refused the statement and insisted on the punishment of Iraq as an aggressor. In recent months, Iraq progressed in the war and returned some territories that were occupied by Iran; it penetrated in the border cities of Iran by using chemical bombs and caused great damage. Iraq still claims that it is ready to accept the statement by the Security Council.

Everybody was so amazed, because until today, they were chanting, "War, War till Victory." They were motivating the forces for twenty years of war. Suddenly everything is changed. The authorities reason that Ayatollah Khomeini made this decision; it was the right time now. He excused himself from any elaboration. Whatever the reason, there is hope for an end to the war. People's reactions were far from expectations. People that suffered for eight years and had many financial and human losses were expecting a victory. They did not express happiness. On the contrary, they were amazed and had a feeling of being cheated. The minimum expectation was to make a referendum on such a great issue, or at least give people advance readiness. The first reaction after acceptance of the statement was the sudden fall of the price of gold and the dollar in the Tehran market. Possibly it was due to the sudden shock of acceptance of the statement. For dispatching soldiers to the front, they were proclaiming vast propaganda on the radio and TV, but on this very important issue that people had sacrificed, many things did not even hint at it.

AUGUST 20, 1988

At last the official ceasefire from eight years of war between Iran and Iraq was signed at the United Nations at 6:30 AM on August 20, 1988. The peace keepers were stationed at the borderlines of the two countries, and the parties respected the rules of the ceasefire. In Iraq, people celebrated and showed their happiness by dancing and singing, but in Iran nothing happened.

The first reaction of the ceasefire was the fall of the price of gold, the dollar and some import commodities. In the first day of the ceasefire, Genaveh port and Khark Island started the export of oil. Very wide projects for renovation of oil establishments started, including the renovation of Abadan Refinery that was the first victim of the Iran–Iraq war.

Western countries are competing for provision of budgets for peace-keeping forces and renovation of the ruins of the war. It seems that development has already started. Contrary to the official declaration of the ceasefire, Iran does not trust Iraq and keeps its forces on the borders in a state of emergency.

Yesterday, Iraq's first oil tanker passed the Hormoz Strait inspected by the Iranian marine force that was protested by Iraq.

As from today, peace negotiations will start at United Nations headquarters. The main points of the meeting are deciding about borderlines of the two countries, the dredging of Shatolarab, and the return of war hostages.

In Iran life is going back to normal, and people have found relative peace of mind. Negotiations will take about six months; until the end, we cannot be sure about incidents.

An important event before the ceasefire between Iran and Iraq was the attack of Mojahedeen Khalgh on Iranian territories which caused heavy damage and their wandering around. Iraq has agreed to give them air coverage and knowingly did not do so. This was the best way Iran and Iraq could get rid of Mojahedin. The group has a bad reputation among Iranians. Iranians will never forgive them for their conspiracy with their enemy.

Western countries declared readiness for investment and trade relations with Iran. It seems that the economy that was working for the war is now working for development and the better living of people. To meet the needs for professional services, the government is expected to review its policy about purification and dismissal.

After the important statement by Imam Khomeini about accepting the ceasefire, no more news was heard of him. Ayatollah Khomeini related the acceptance of the ceasefire to drinking a glass of poison. He promised to give the reason later on, but he never did so.

JUNE 4, 1988

Today Ayatollah Khomeini passed away from cancer. His body was placed for one day in the Great Mosala of Tehran for a farewell. The ceremony was so crowded that the staff could not perform the proper ceremony. As soon as the news was spread, people came to Tehran from all over the country to Jamaran (Khomeini's resident) and Mosala. They were throwing themselves to reach the body. The special prayer for the deceased faced many problems. When the body was ready to be sent to the Behesht Zahra Cemetery, huge crowds made movement of the ambulance impossible. The same crowd gathered in Behesht Zahra. Helicopters were flying over Behesht Zahra and could not land. The process was shown live on TV. Due to the great crowds, the funeral did not get performed the proper way for a leader.

The government announced one week of public holiday and forty days of public mourning. After a few hours, the Experts Assembly was held, and Khamenei was elected leader. Every day groups of people from different provinces went to Jamaran (resident of Ayatollah Khomeini) to show sympathy to his family. The city is covered with black cloths and mourning slogans.

A few days after the passing of Ayatollah Khomeini, Rafsanjani, the Parliament chair and substitute for

Ayatollah Khomeini as commander in chief, went to Russia on a pre-planned program and was very much welcomed. He visited Gorbachev and signed important treaties, including the sale of gas and receiving permits from Russia to export gas to the other countries through Russia.

On the matter of Afghanistan, the two leaders agreed not to interfere in that country and let people work on their own destiny. In the cities with Muslim populations, Rafsanjani was most welcomed. He said "I feel to be among my own people." This successful trip made some ease in the situation.

The Western world is worried about the close relationship between Iran and Russia. Iran prefers to have better relations with its north neighbor. Rafsanjani said, "Ayatollah Khomeini recommended good relations."

Election of the president will start soon because the present president became the leader. Among all the candidates the strongest is Rafsanjani. People hope change in the constitution will result in a better environment.

This year's trip to Mecca for Iranian pilgrims was not possible. Saudi Arabia portioned a number of pilgrims and was doing repair works in Mecca. This was not acceptable to the Iranian government.

A vast land with urban establishments is foreseen for the tomb of Ayatollah Khomeini. The facilities will include a pilgrim residence, health department, schools, etc. Engineers and workers are working fast to make it ready for visitors on the fortieth day of passing away. They expect the place to be a sacred place for Muslims. People donated for the building, and the government made all facilities to finish it quickly. They have prepared a special piece of prayer for entering the shrine.

Now people are hopeful and expect to have a better living when the president is elected. In the black market, the price of the dollar reduced from 140 Tomans to 100 Tomans, which caused a change in imported commodities and real estate.

I stop writing this memoir and hope the days I reported never happen again in this country.

OCTOBER, 2008

At the end I would like to tell you about my own life.

Before the law on "Purification of Government Employees" was to be ratified, I was laid off while I was retired from service in the Central Bank of Iran. The Revolutionary Court condemned me to strengthening the base of the ex-regime and a punishment of paying back all salaries and allowances I made during my service in high jobs. They cut the retirement money that I was paid during my years of service. For ten years, I was forbidden to travel out of the country and was called to the Revolutionary Court many times. They could not find any wrongdoing in my record.

As I was permitted by the Ministry of Justice to make official translations from Farsi to English and vice-versa, I started a translation office called "Takht-e Tavoos" and translated the documents of students and people that intended to go abroad. I also did translation of documents between the Iranian government and people from English-speaking countries. As people were in a hurry to go out of the country, my business was booming, and my income exceeded the money I used to receive as a government employee. After paying all the money that they asked for, they let me go.

Mina, my daughter, and her husband, Mohammad

Fotovat, and their children had immigrated to Canada. My husband and I went to Canada on their support. It is now twenty-two years that I have been in Toronto and was accepted with very welcome remarks by the immigration officer.

My grandchildren, Nima, Sahba, and Salma, are well educated and have a very successful business under the management of their father. Mina is an official translator with a good reputation and skills in her job.

In Toronto, I started social volunteer work and established the Iranian Women's Organization of Ontario, which is a very active and well-known organization and renders many services to newcomers and Iranian families. This organization provides educational workshops, health services, legal advice, referral services, childcare, English classes, and summer camps for seniors. The government of Canada recognizes the organization and supports its programs.

I also started the Iranian Canadian Senior Citizens Organization that provides many services to Iranian seniors. And I helped the Canadian Afghan Center for War-affected Children to be established and start working.

Recently a study was done by the Ministry of Women's Affairs Intercultural Network about senior women over sixty-five years who have performed volunteer work in their own countries and in Canada. Among seniors of all countries, they selected seven women and their biographies; CDs from their interviews were sent to schools for children. I was one of the seven women who received the award.

I have a pleasant life in Canada and receive a senior's pension. During the years in Canada, I have written many articles about women, children, and seniors and given many lectures in Farsi and in English about the situation of women in Iran.

I have two books for translation in my hands. One is about the wonderful management of a woman during the Second World War; the other is about two children affected by an earthquake in Greece, and the way they were survived. I hope I can finish these books.

Recently I made a trip to Iran and was surprised with the changes. The city looked cleaner. Many high-rises were built, and the view of the city has completely changed. Everybody complains about high prices and pollution. Traffic in Tehran is so complicated; all main and subsidiary roads are mostly closed and pedestrians move between vehicles. Every day, hours of people's time are wasted in traffic, and people are always late.

Iranian women have problems with Islamic hijab. The government has forces to watch them. They punish those who do not consider proper covering, which makes a bad record for them. Women resistance is wonderful. In my view, they are a beautiful generation full of energy and initiation. With all hard times that they are facing, they appear in streets with full make-up and colorful scarves and do not care for the rules. I think it is a kind of struggle for obtaining freedom and the equality of rights.

From a political view, people are well informed and have their own views. Those who benefit from the government's privileges enjoy their life. The others work several shifts to survive. Everybody expects a miracle that does not happen. Now Iran is involved with the enrichment of uranium. The world is trying to prevent Iran from such an activity. Super powers have tough sanctions on Iran that have direct effect on people's lives.

Apparently high prices of gas and food are a universal problem.

God knows what will happen next. I'm hoping better days for Iranian people, especially women that are working hard for equality and freedom.

THE END

Order by Shahbanu Farah Pahlavi appointment of Homa Rouhi as
a Board Member of National Association for Helping Children.
June 1972

فرح پهلوی

باستناد ماده سوّاساسنامهٔ انجمن ملی حمایت کودکان بموجب این تنظا

باوهاروحی دسرشتی، رابرای مدّت پنجسال بسمت عضو محمع عمومی انجمن نامبرده

منصوب میداریم .   بتاریخ خرداد ماه یکهزار و سیصد و پنجاه و یک ۱۳۵۱

مهم بودی

Order by Shahbanu Farah Pahlavi

248

Letter by Princess Asharaf Pahlavi recognizing services rendered by Homa Rouhi to Iranian Women.   March 19, 1977

اشرف پهلوی

جناب بانو هما روحی

عضو شورای مرکزی سازمان زنان ایران

بپاس خدمات ارزنده ای که برای پیشرفت امور سازمان زنان ایران انجام

داده اید بدینوسیله مراتب رضامندی خود را ابراز می نمایم .

تاریخ هشتم اسفند ماه ۲۵۳۶

ریاست عالیه

Letter by Princess Ashraf Pahlavi

Homa Rouhi (Sarlati)

Order by Shah of Iran appointing Homa Rouhi to Board of
Trustees of Farah Pahlavi University. December 1975

طبق پیشنهاد وزیر علوم و آموزش عالی، و به استناد اساسنامه دانشگاه فرح پهلوی و بوجبان

خانم روحی را برای مدت سه سال بعضویت هیئت امناء دانشگاه مزبور منصوب و مقرر میدارم

که دستگاه اجرای طبق نظم محل به اقدام نماید. کاخ نیاوران . بتاریخ نهم دیماه ۱۳۵۴ شمسی

Order by Shah of Iran

FAMILY SERVICE ASSOCIATION

recognizes the volunteer
contributions of

Homa Sarlati

Illahee Lodge Seniors' Wellness / Health Promotion Programs

this day *24th* *of* *June* , *1998*

Executive Director

President, Board of Directors

Letter by Family Services Association-Toronto

The Iranian-Canadian Network
for Employment and Entrepreneurship Mentoring

The Board of Directors of I.C. Network

Extends their heartfelt thanks to

Ms. Homa Sarlati

Acknowledging a community activist who has made an outstanding contribution
toward improving the quality of life of
Iranian-Canadian women
We thank you for the important role that you play in
the Iranian-Canadian community

On behalf of the Board of Directors
Ramtin Sotoadeh, P. Eng.
Chairperson

30th September 2004

Letter by Iranian Canadian Network for Employment and
Entrepreneurship Mentoring

THE WOMEN'S INTERCULTURAL NETWORK

Presents its

PERSON'S DAY AWARD

To

HOMA ROUHI-SARLATI

*Lawyer, Banker, Researcher, Deputy Minister,
Champion of Human Rights.*

*October 18, 2007
Toronto, Ontario*

Letter by The Women Intercultural Network

CITY OF
TORONTO

Mayor Mel Lastman
and Members of Toronto City Council
extend their heartfelt thanks to

Homa Sarlati

in honour of your outstanding contribution
as a volunteer.

Volunteers are the heart and soul of our warm and
caring City. As a volunteer, you can be extremely
proud of the important role you play every day and
the support you provide to your organization.

Your dedication, enthusiasm, tireless efforts and your
generous gift of time, have made a real difference in
many lives and made our City a better place to
work, live and play.

As we celebrate the International Year of
Volunteers in 2001, we thank you for caring and
giving. You are one of the reasons why Toronto is the
greatest City in the world!

Mayor Mel Lastman

2001
International Year
of Volunteers

City of Toronto Mayor - Mel Lastman

International Year
of Volunteers

*In Honour
of your Volunteer
Contribution*

2001

Année internationale
des volontaires

*En hommage
à votre contribution
bénévole*

Homa Sarlati

Thank you for
helping to strengthen
your community
and province

 Ontario

Merci d'aider
à fortifier
votre collectivité et
votre province

The Honourable Cam Jackson / L'honorable Cam Jackson
Minister of Citizenship / Ministre des Affaires civiques

Ministry of Citizenship

تقدیرنامه

بدینوسیله مراتب سپاس و قدردانی خود را از کمکهای ارزشمند

سرکار خانم هما سرلتی

رسان به اهداف نیکوکارانه بنیاد کهریزک، صمیمانه ابراز میداریم و این لوح تقدیر به رسم تقدیم میگردد.

Certificate of Appreciation

Ms. Homa Sarlati

In Recognition of Exemplary Contribution To

Kahrizak Foundation
Toronto, Canada

President

Committee of Public A...

Kahrizak Charity Foundation

Homa Rouhi (Sarlati)

UNITED NATIONS
ECONOMIC AND SOCIAL COMMISSION
FOR ASIA AND THE PACIFIC (ESCAP)
THIRTY-FIRST SESSION, NEW DELHI
26 FEBRUARY - 7 MARCH 1975
HOMA ROUHI
IRAN

UNITED NATIONS

DELEGATION

VALID TO 5/4/78 ___ Conference __Status of Women__

M_H.E. Mrs. Homa ROHHI_

OF __IRAN__

__Chairman of the Delegation__

NO. 1A-320

BMS.55.G/B

Chief of Protocol

Participation in the United Nations Meetings

www.ingramcontent.com/pod-product-compliance
Lightning Source LLC
Chambersburg PA
CBHW030257290526
45785CB00001B/119